D1385658

ABOUT THE AUTHOR

DR LAURA MEEK has worked as a doctor in the NHS since 2007 and has an interest in empowering young people to take charge of their own mental health. She draws on her experience of working in Child and Adolescent Mental Health Services alongside elements of cognitive behavioural therapy and mindfulness to help children to become their very own superheroes. Laura lives in Yorkshire with her husband and two children.

DR LAURA MEEK

BE YOUR OWN SUPERHERO

Illustrated by JAMES DAVIES

PUFFIN

PUFFIN BOOKS

UK | USA | Canada | Ireland | Australia
India | New Zealand | South Africa

Puffin Books is part of the Penguin Random House group of companies
whose addresses can be found at global.penguinrandomhouse.com.

www.penguin.co.uk
www.puffin.co.uk
www.ladybird.co.uk

Penguin Random House UK

First published 2019

001

Text and illustrations copyright © Penguin Books Ltd, 2019
Foreword copyright © Nikesh Shukla, 2019
Text by Laura Meek
Illustrations by James Davies
Text design by Janene Spencer

Printed and bound in Great Britain by Clays Ltd, Elcograf S.p.A

A CIP catalogue record for this book is available from the British Library

ISBN: 978-0-241-41741-6

All correspondence to:
Puffin Books
Penguin Random House Children's
80 Strand, London WC2R ORL

CONTENTS

FOREWORD
BY NIKESH SHUKLA

'People like us . . . we don't get a choice.'
Spider-Man, *the Amazing Spider-Man Annual #35*

The world needs superheroes. Now more than ever. It will be those of you holding this book in your hands who will change the world. That's amazing, right? But I know that can feel scary too.

We already have so much going on in our own lives it can be hard to find space to help others. But it's important to remember that everything helps, whether it's big or small. A random act of kindness, showing someone you're thinking about them, stopping a runaway train with your bare hands . . . All of these make you a superhero.

I was obsessed with Spider-Man while growing up. I totally got Peter Parker's dual identity – one moment the science nerd, the other a web-slinging hero. I totally got the way he switched between shyness in one life and cockiness in the other. He wore different

masks and spoke in different languages in different situations. Often, while trying to do good, he was caught in lies. He led a secret life. He was unpopular at school. He could have been me.

I kept my head down at school and studied hard, trying my best not to fail at the subjects my father longed for me to succeed in – science and maths – while doing well at English and creative writing. My dad didn't really care about those two things. I spoke in different languages: slang with my friends, quietly and as posh as I could with my teachers (because if I didn't, I had learned that people automatically assumed I didn't speak English), and gangster rap in my head.

I felt that same sense of responsibility as Peter Parker too. I was going to be the first person in my family to go to university and so the pressure was on for me to do well. Except, Dad didn't really care about the subjects I was doing well in. So I turned to comic books to help me understand the world.

The idea of putting on a suit and being a better version of yourself appealed to me because I didn't feel particularly powerful most of the time. For Superman, putting on his suit meant being himself (Clark Kent being the everyday mask he wore); for Spider-Man, putting on his suit meant being everything Peter Parker couldn't be. I found comfort in that. In life I was Peter Parker – reading comics, I was Spider-Man. I dreamed of the confidence with which Spider-Man dispensed of Doctor Octopus or the Green Goblin; the boldness with which he deployed his web-shooters; the wisecracks he flung at villains with abandon. These were characters who struggled to have the bravery to do the right thing, to keep going when it looked like there wasn't hope, to manage their emotions and make the world a better place for other people. But they always triumphed in the end. Now I've grown up and I have kids of my own, that's all I want for them too.

That's why the book you're about to read will help you hone your own skills. Because it shows that we all have the ability to develop superpowers – maybe not to swing between buildings, or leap

across tall buildings in a single bound – but to learn how to listen to other people, to think about where they are coming from, to find the confidence to be ourselves, to handle our negative emotions and doubts, and to keep going.

As an adult, I fight for people who are vulnerable and powerless, and I use my voice and my actions to stand up for them.

Like Uncle Ben once said to Peter Parker, with great power comes great responsibility. We all have superpowers within us. And we have to channel them for good. Because the world is made up of what we put into it and what we take from it. This book will help you work out what you can do because you can make a difference in people's lives. We all can. It's time for you to become **a superhero**.

INTRODUCTION

When you find yourself in a sticky situation, do you look to the skies for someone to swoop in and help you? Or would you rather use your own superpowers to save the day?

Knew it.

You want to be a superhero, don't you?

Cool!

But be warned: it's not just as simple as doing push-ups, pull-ups and all the other -ups.

Still interested?

Great! You've passed the first test – a superhero never gives up. This book will help you earn your superhero cape (all the best superheroes have capes, right?) and I'm here to guide you along the way. I can't tell you much about myself because I'm a superhero too, and must protect my secret identity . . . All you need to know

is that you've probably heard of me.[1] I'm going to share everything I've learned about my own powers and from my superhero friends with you in this book. Lucky you!

First of all, good news: the only thing you need to be a superhero is yourself! You might not realize it yet, but you have a superhero inside yourself just waiting to be discovered!

You've probably already caught some glimpses of your inner superhero before. Ever had a tingling, nervous feeling in your belly when you've had to do something you're really worried about, but you've still managed to do it? Or what about a lovely warm feeling when you've done something kind for someone else without being asked? These things are excellent examples of your strong, considerate **inner superhero**.

In this book, you'll uncover all sorts of cool superpowers and skills! You'll learn how to read people's minds using **telepathy**, become a **shape-shifter** by working on your **flexible thinking** and even build up your **super strength** by exercising your body and your mind! What's more,

---

[1] Or maybe not, but please don't tell me that – I may be a superhero but I'm still vulnerable to harsh words.

you'll learn about the four elements we all have within us – **fire**, **water**, **air** and **earth** – and how to control and balance each of them using your thoughts and feelings.

With a bit of practice, you'll soon have your superpowers mastered. Training your powers can be tough sometimes, though. You don't get to be Batman or Wonder Woman without a bit of work, after all. But don't worry, I've tried to make things as easy as possible.

Each chapter focuses on a specific superpower and in every one you'll find ideas and activities for practising that power.

SUPERHERO TIPS

Throughout the book, my superhero friends will pop up with ideas for activities you can try to practise your powers. Some are small things your INNER HERO can do to help you feel happier, more confident and more in control of your emotions. Others are little ways your OUTER HERO can thrive by making a difference to your family, friends and the wider world. When you put your superpowers to excellent use, the sky's the limit!

You can read the chapters in any order, a chapter at a time, whenever you want – just pick up the book, then try out an activity. I promise all your hard work will pay off!

Of course, there's one very important thing that every superhero needs: **a trusty sidekick** – or several! Make sure you surround yourself with people you love and trust, as they'll help you with your superhero transformation.

The coolest thing about becoming your own superhero is that it's really all about being yourself. You don't need to go around beating up baddies[2] or wearing a mask.[3] The best feeling comes from seeing all your hard work pay off, and that's a feeling that only comes from **inside you**.

Before we get stuck in, you need to choose a **cool superhero name** for yourself! If you need some ideas, think of something you're really good at and start from there. Your name could even be about your favourite superpower. You don't have to tell anyone else what your superhero name is, if you don't want to – it can be your secret. Right, what are we waiting for?

---

[2] And it's not a good idea to beat anyone up!
[3] You don't even have to wear a mask if you don't want to. (Rogue from X-Men never bothered. She went with a pretty cool hairdo instead.)

LET'S GET STARTED!

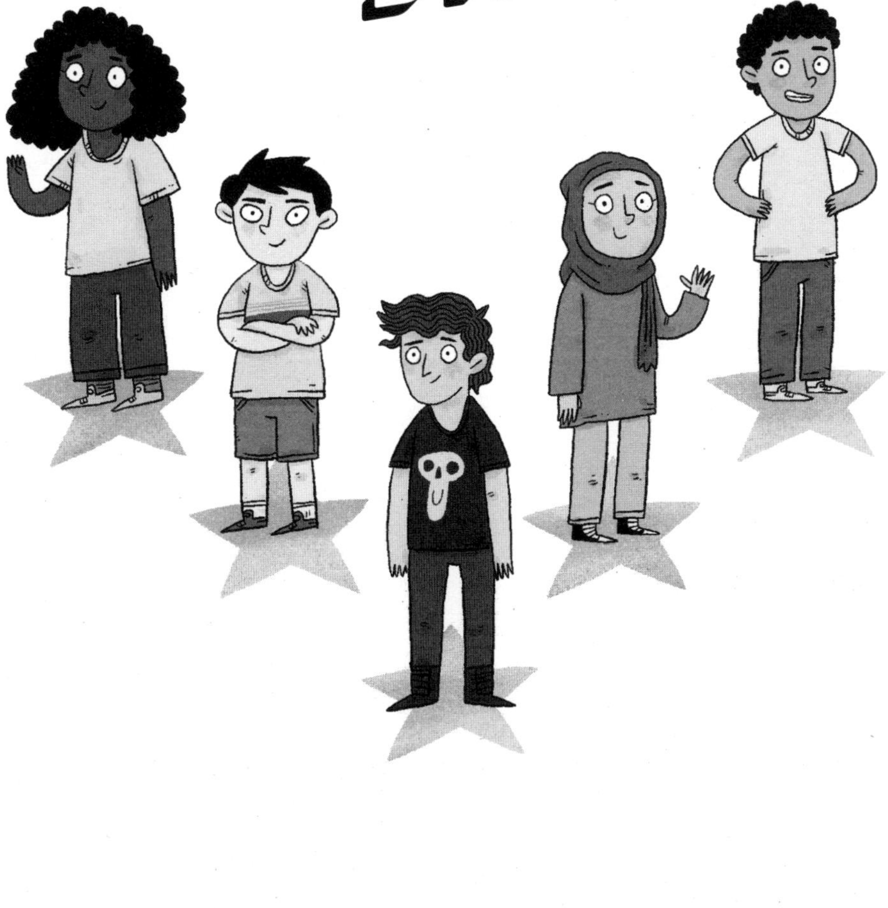

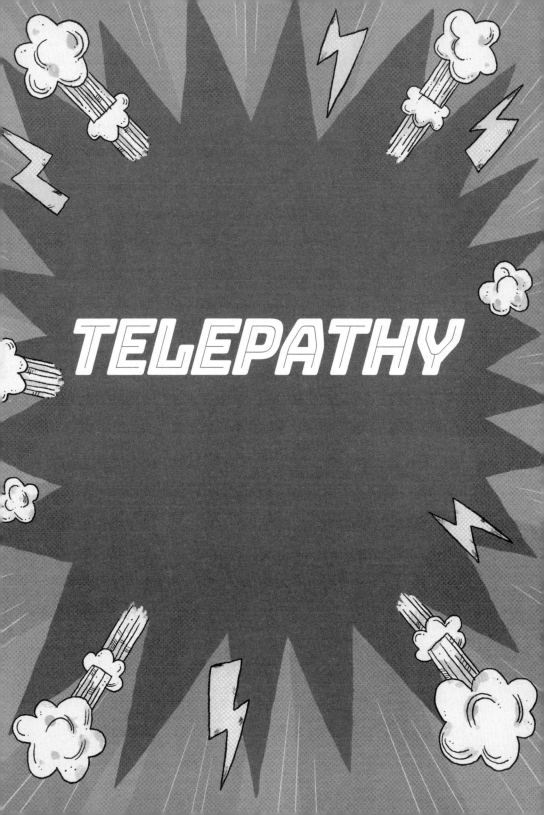

You've heard of telepathy, right? If not, don't worry. You're going to know all about it very soon! Once you've mastered it, you'll be able to use your **telepathic superpower** to work out what other people are thinking or feeling without them having to say a word. This is an extra-useful superpower to have because understanding what other people are thinking or feeling will help you know how best to respond to them.

You might think others see things exactly the same as you – that the things that make you sad or happy or angry make other people feel that way too – but this isn't true. Here's the truth: **we all feel different things for all sorts of different reasons**. The thing that makes one person really happy – maybe it's bugs and beetles (yes, some people do like them!) – could be the same thing that makes you squirm with fear.

This is where the superpower of telepathy comes in handy. If you can read another person's mind, you'll be able to understand why they're behaving in a particular way – even if it's not the same way you'd behave in that situation, or the way you'd like that person to act. When you can read someone's mind, it gets a lot easier to understand why they behave in a certain way.

MIND-READING BASICS

Telepathy can be a tricky business, so let's start with the basics.

First of all, think of someone you know who behaves very differently from you. For example, if you are naturally quiet, it could be someone who loves to talk. Or if you tend to smile a lot, it might be someone who always seems to be scowling.

Think about why that person might be behaving so differently from you. In the case of the scowl-face, you might assume they're scowling because they're really annoyed – and maybe they are![1] But now ask yourself how you react when you see someone who looks really grumpy. Do you:

- **smile at first, then stop when they don't return your smile?**
- **avoid them altogether, because they look miserable?**
- **make zero effort to talk to them, because you assume they're unfriendly?**

Hmm . . . when you look at it like that, scowling seems like a

---

[1] Whenever I used to get annoyed, my mum would warn me to be careful or my face would 'stick like that' – and that was enough to keep me looking grumpy for at least a day!

pretty good way to keep other people away. There's a whole bunch of reasons why someone might want to do that.

Perhaps they're very shy, or maybe they find it really difficult to talk to others. A person who is scowling all the time might not actually be annoyed. They might just be having a bad day, or things in their life might be especially tough at the moment – you never know what someone else has going on, after all. Or perhaps they just have a face that looks a bit grumpy, even if all they're doing is daydreaming and they have no idea they're scowling!

As your telepathy superpower grows stronger, you'll get better at spotting clues to help you work out exactly what could be going on beneath a person's scowl and other expressions. Remember that **what you see on the outside isn't always how someone is actually feeling on the inside**.

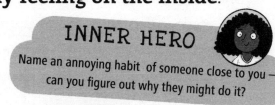

INNER HERO

Name an annoying habit of someone close to you – can you figure out why they might do it?

On the outside, someone may look like this.

But actually, on the inside, they feel like this.

It's really important to remember when mind-reading that someone's past experiences can have a **big impact on how they react to things**. Keeping this in mind when someone is behaving differently from how you would behave can help you to understand that person and think about how to respond to them. It can also help you to become aware of yourself and your own actions. So if you love swimming, for example, but your best friend can't swim, it might help if you understood why they feel a little scared of water. Knowing this would help you to be considerate of their feelings and not rush them into doing something they're not comfortable with – or push them into a pool!

Sometimes, you might know about someone's past experiences, but at other times you'll have to use your telepathy to try to make a guess. And always remember that you'll never, ever know exactly what's gone and is going on in another person's life. These things might affect someone's behaviour:

FAMILY ENVIRONMENT

When a person is part of a loving family and has supportive friends around them, the world isn't such a scary place and it's so much easier to trust others. It can help someone feel more confident about taking risks, because they know there's a team there to cheer them on.

But someone without that kind of safe and happy family environment might find the world a lonely and frightening place - certainly enough to make them scowl.

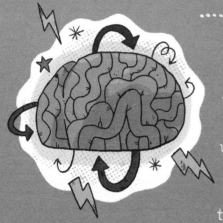

PAST EXPERIENCES OF A SIMILAR SITUATION

The human brain loves to make patterns and connections! If we feel happy when we do something for the first time, we're more likely to think it will always be a fun experience. Unfortunately, the opposite can be true after a bad experience - we'll probably be scared of doing it again.

LIKES AND DISLIKES

Thanks to our unique personalities, every single one of us has our own preferences. If a situation particularly appeals to our likes, we're more likely to be supportive or excited about it. But the opposite applies when someone dislikes what they're experiencing. If they don't like what's happening, they might be nervous or negative about it, which could be very different from how you're feeling.

So the next time you're in a situation where you feel someone else isn't responding or behaving how you'd like them to, try to imagine all the reasons why they might be acting as they are, even if you don't know for sure. Telepathy isn't about finding out the answers. Just by considering how all sorts of things might be impacting someone else's actions, you're using your superpower to be a kinder, more thoughtful person!

EXTRA-SENSORY PERCEPTION (ESP)

ESP is really cool! It's almost like a sixth sense that can help you to work out how someone else is feeling and what they might be thinking. It basically combines telepathy and enhanced senses and the more you use ESP the better you'll get at it.

You can engage your ESP by keeping the following questions in mind when you're talking to someone.

WHAT IS THEIR BODY LANGUAGE LIKE?

Are they smiling and looking at you, or are they looking downwards? Think about how you act when you're happy, and then when you're sad. Are they doing any of those same things?

AM I LISTENING?

Sometimes, someone will come right out and tell you how they feel, but you just don't hear it! Learning to listen - really hearing what someone's saying - is so important. It can help you to be a better friend. Make sure you look at them while they're talking, to show that you're giving them your full attention. Don't daydream, and don't interrupt them. If you want to make sure that you've understood them properly, try repeating what they've told you back to them, using your own words.

WHAT DO I ALREADY KNOW ABOUT THEM?

Maybe you know that your friend has just lost their beloved pet. Or perhaps they scored the winning goal in the hockey match at the weekend. This is the sort of information that can give you some pretty good clues about how your friend might be feeling.

All right, now that you've got the basics of telepathy and ESP, let's look at how you can start to put your superpower into practice! You're ready to begin using it to react kindly and thoughtfully to any situation, and to show others you care about their emotions. This is also called 'showing empathy', which means being able to understand and imagine how another person is feeling.

OUTER HERO

Think of a task at home that your parents always ask you to do – like making your bed or taking out the rubbish. Try and do it without being asked for a whole week and see how your parents react!

TELEPATHY IN ACTION

Sometimes when our friends or loved ones are experiencing strong feelings – like being really happy or really sad – we feel some of their feelings, too. We imagine we are in their situation, and how that would feel for us. I'm sure you've done this before! Have you ever told another person that you were feeling for them in this way? How did they respond? Lots of times, other people find it comforting when we show them empathy like this. It's nice to have someone else show that they care!

Sometimes, showing empathy and being thoughtful of another person's feelings means putting your own feelings to the side for a bit.

Here's a story about Charlie and Jay. One day outside school, Charlie spotted their friend Jay sitting on the wall and looking sad. It was already 3.30 p.m. and Charlie knew that, even if they left right now, they'd barely make it home in time for their favourite TV show to start. However, Charlie also knew that Jay's parents had recently got divorced, and as a result Jay had moved to a new house. In that moment, Charlie had a choice.

1. THEY COULD HAVE SHOUTED TO JAY, 'BYE! SEE YOU TOMORROW! SORRY, CAN'T STOP.'

Then, they could have walked home super quickly and would have made it back just in time. They'd had a busy day at school, after all, and they really just wanted to relax.

2. OR, THEY COULD STOP AND ASK JAY HOW HE WAS FEELING.

They would be able to catch up on their show later. Right now, talking to their friend seemed more important – Charlie could only imagine how hard it must be for Jay, moving house and having to split his time between his parents. Jay looked so sad, and Charlie knew that they would want him to stop and talk to them if they felt like that.

I'm sure you can tell which option Charlie chose, because they were using their telepathy superpower! In situations like this, it's important to stop and think about how you would feel if you were the other person. Doing this engages your telepathy, and helps you to become a better friend. What's more, you never know how much a kind gesture might mean to someone else – it might just help to make their life a little bit happier.

What would you do if you were Charlie?

Would you leave Jay sad on that wall, or would you try to help him with a caring word, a listening ear or a fun activity? If you ever find yourself in a similar situation, but you don't know what you can do, here are some things you can try.

- Give the person a hug. Just remember to ask them if they want one first – not all of us like physical contact!
- Listen to them, and give them a chance to talk about how they feel.
- Plan something fun together that will help to take their mind off things.
- Make them a gift. You could bake a cake or make a card, then give it to them when you see them next.

There's one very important thing to remember here: **it is OK to be sad sometimes**. No one is happy all the time, and sometimes we have very good reason to be sad. This applies to everyone – including you.

OUTER HERO

Next time you notice a friend looking sad or annoyed, ask them what's wrong. Listen carefully and give them a hug if they want one.

THINGS TO AVOID

So far, we've looked at some ideas for what you might do to help, but it is also good to know **what not to do**. It's worth knowing what could make things worse, so that you can avoid doing it.

Take a moment to think of a time when you felt as though you weren't being understood. Why did you feel that way, do you think? When we feel misunderstood, it's often because of someone's reaction to us.

Here are some things to avoid, so that someone else doesn't feel as though you don't understand or care about them.

INNER HERO

Try and pinpoint something that you do that others might not like. Can you figure out why you act that way and – even better – think of how you can change it?

STAY AWAY FROM SARCASM.

When you are sarcastic, you say one thing but you really mean another. People use it to sound funny, but it can be confusing. If you use it when someone is angry or upset, they can feel as though you don't care.

AVOID ONE-UPMANSHIP.

When you one-up someone, you try to outdo them. Sometimes, people do this by telling a story that is far worse or more interesting or more dramatic than another person's. If you do this, it can leave the other person feeling as though the conversation is actually a competition. They might also feel that what they've said wasn't interesting enough – or that you didn't really hear it.

DON'T BRUSH THINGS OFF.

A lot of times, people will try to make someone feel better by saying, 'It could be worse.' However, if you do this, it can mean the other person just feels like you aren't taking them seriously.

DON'T TRY TO OFFER A SOLUTION.

That's not your job. Other people don't always want an answer, and they don't want to feel like a problem to be solved. All they want is for you to listen.

WITH GREAT POWER COMES GREAT RESPONSIBILITY

All right, there's just one more thing we have to cover before you start using your telepathy superpower: you need to know that there are some times when you **shouldn't use it**. That sounds strange, right? What's the point in learning all about telepathy, if you're not going to be able to use it? Well, it's not as bizarre as you may think! Let me explain.

Everything you've learned about so far is stuff that you do inside your own head. For the most part, you don't actually say anything to another person about what you think they want or feel. You simply use your telepathy to empathize with them, and to make an informed decision about how to react.

It's really important to know that, in certain circumstances, you must ask someone how they think and feel about something **before you do anything**. You might think that you know how they feel or what they want, but you can't be sure unless you ask them.

This is especially important when it comes to any sort of physical contact with another person. Do not touch another person unless they have said, yes, they are happy for you to do so. Every single one of us has the right to say yes or no to being touched. You might love a big hug, but it can make some people feel uncomfortable! Even if someone says yes at the start, they might change their mind part-way through – maybe the hug is going on just a bit too long for them. This is fine too; we all have the right to say **'stop'** if something makes us feel uncomfortable.

It's actually really easy to ask for permission. All you have to do is ask something like, 'Is it OK if I give you a hug?' If the person says yes, then go right ahead and give them a great big hero hug. (Just don't squeeze too tight – remember your super strength!) If they say no, that's no big deal. It's their choice. **Respect it, and move on.** It doesn't mean they don't care about you – it's just their preference in that moment.

So, now you know exactly when and how to engage your telepathy. You may go forth and read minds! You'll soon realize you're a better friend, sibling, child (or anything else!) thanks to your new superpower.

OUTER HERO

Try out your telepathy on animals! If you have a friend or family member with a dog that would enjoy being outside more, could you offer to take it for a walk?

A vital skill in your journey to superhero-dom is learning all about your fire power, and how to control one aspect of it in particular: **anger**. This is a vital superhero skill – you'll use it a lot! It's also a big responsibility.

Basically, you're going to learn how to not let your fire power take control of your actions. You might find this a bit tricky to master, but it just takes practice. Have you ever seen the Human Torch completely lose it? Of course not! He's obviously put in lots of **practice with his superpowers**.

Like all emotions, anger is a normal feeling. We all get angry sometimes. When you get angry, it can feel as though your whole body is heating up like a kettle full of boiling water. The hot emotion

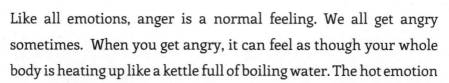

bubbles away inside you, making all that steam build up, until it eventually feels like you're going to **explode**! An explosion of anger has pretty much the same effect as a kettle that boils over: all that hot water and steam escapes, making a huge mess and usually hurting someone. It can leave you and everyone around you pretty miserable.

When you feel the first bubbles of anger heating up inside you, you can choose one of two options: you can let yourself get so angry that you boil over and explode, or you can turn down the heat and let yourself cool down. To control your fire power, you need to be able to **recognize the signs** that anger is starting to build in your body, so that you can turn the temperature down.

Another way to think of anger is like a mountain. As anger builds in your body, you climb higher and higher. The idea is to try to recognize the signs of the anger before you reach the peak. If your heart is racing and you're not thinking clearly any more, then you've already reached the top of **Anger Mountain**. Controlling your anger at the summit of the mountain can be a little trickier than if you realize it earlier, on the way up, but you're about to learn some tricks that will help you climb back down that mountain and regain control.

USE YOUR TEMPERATURE CONTROL

Did you know that anger isn't just a feeling or an emotion? It's also a physical response to a situation that happens inside your body. When your brain senses that you are feeling anger, it thinks it's time for action, so it sends signals to other parts of your body to get ready. For example, it gets your heart to beat faster and pump more blood to your muscles so they can get ready to help you run or fight if needed.

Anger isn't always a bad thing. In fact, it can sometimes be pretty amazing. It can motivate you and give you passion. It can help you to get stuff done. Don't believe me? Here are some examples of people doing anger right.

- 'I was angry that our local library was closing, so I wrote to my local MP about it.'
- 'I was angry that I missed the goal in our football match, so I practised even harder to make sure it wouldn't happen again.'

Pretty awesome work, huh?[1] But we all know that anger can also totally suck. Any of these situations ring a bell?

- **'My little brother took my favourite game without asking. I felt so angry. We got into a fight, and I accidentally hurt his arm.'**
- **'I couldn't do my science homework. It was just too hard. I felt angry that I couldn't remember everything from class, so I ripped up my workbook.'**

There's an important difference between these two sets of examples. Did you catch what it was? The difference is what each person *did* with their anger. In the first set of examples, both people engaged their fire power and channelled their anger into doing something helpful – they used it to motivate them to write a letter, or to practice harder. On the flip side, in the second set of examples, both people let their anger get out of control and then their actions ended up being unhelpful (and a bit dangerous).

---

[1] Not as awesome as me being so angry at myself that I practised teleporting all week . . . I am currently in Disneyland, but *technically* I am still grounded.

To really start to control your fire power, you need to learn what makes you angry in the first place. For most people, anger is caused by either not getting what they want (you really want to go to the park but it's raining), or getting what they *don't* want (your mum serves you soup, your least favourite meal, for lunch).

Sounds pretty simple when you put it like that, right?

Now, think about the last few times you felt angry. For each one, ask yourself the following questions:

- **What made me angry?**
- **How did I feel – both in my head, and in my body?**
- **How did I react? What did I do?**
- **Was my reaction helpful, or was it unhelpful?**

Asking these questions will help you to start to understand a bit more about why you get angry about things, and what some of the warning signs are.

FLAME...
OR INFERNO?

When it comes to thinking and feeling, there are two parts of your brain that play different roles. As you can see in the diagram, your higher brain is the smart bit – it thinks about things and makes decisions. Your lower brain is the impulsive bit, which means that it reacts to things without thinking about them. Your lower brain kicks in and just does things based on instinct, while your higher brain does things after giving them some thought.

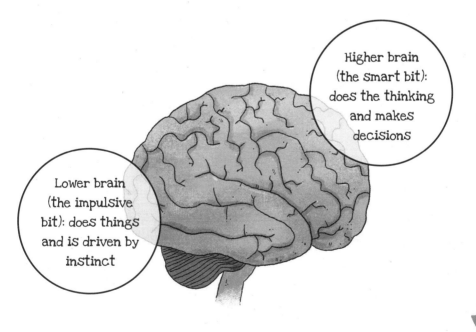

Higher brain (the smart bit): does the thinking and makes decisions

Lower brain (the impulsive bit): does things and is driven by instinct

When we feel angry, we have a choice about which part of our brain we listen to: our higher brain or our lower brain. Both parts are important, but when it comes to anger it's better not to let your lower brain take charge – otherwise, before you know it, you'll be dealing with a raging-hot anger inferno![2] Your calm and sensible higher brain is like a fire extinguisher that helps to control the angry flames.[3]

Sometimes, though, your impulsive brain can be pretty useful. It helps to release adrenaline, which is what your body uses when you feel scared to make you big and strong – a very good thing if you are in danger and you need to run away *fast*. Just be warned: when there's all that focus on the action, there's not much energy left for thinking. So, you might be able to run fast . . . but are you running the right way? Thanks a lot, brain!

---

[2] This is one of those huge fires you sometimes see on TV. They're really hot - if you see one, don't go near it . . . I spent a year growing my hair back last time I got too close.

[3] It'd make superheroes' jobs so much easier if adults would just learn how to use fire extinguishers properly . . . There wouldn't be nearly as many burning buildings to save people from!

I'm pretty sure you wouldn't want to be known as The Superhero Who Runs Into Walls When They Get Angry! So, what you really want is for both parts of your brain to be working together. Use that fire extinguisher to keep the fire power at a gentle burn rather than a full-on inferno. Don't let that fire get out of control by making sure that your smart brain is in charge of your impulsive brain! When you learn how to control the fire, you learn how to manage your anger.

TURN DOWN THE FLAMES

Learning to control your fire power takes some real practice. Do you remember those questions you asked yourself about things you have felt angry about (page 32)? Now, think about those same times when you were angry, but this time ask yourself:

- **How did my body feel when I was angry?**
- **Was my inferno brain or my fire-extinguisher brain in charge?**

Often, we can see signs that someone feels angry from how they appear on the outside. They might become red in the face, clench their fists and have an unhappy expression. Did you notice any of these things when you thought about how your body felt when you were angry? If so, that's ace! You've already got to know your body a bit better.

A big part of controlling your fire power is being able to realize when you're heating up by spotting your body's warning signs.

Feels like hitting something

Face getting hot

Heart racing

Fists clenching

Of course, anger isn't just something that shows on the outside. Since it's an emotion, you also feel it on the inside. It can make you want to hit or break something, and it can even cause changes in your body that other people can't see. You might feel your heart beating fast – this is a result of all that adrenaline flying round inside your body, getting you ready to fight or to run.

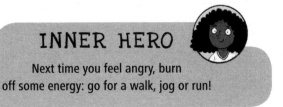

INNER HERO

Next time you feel angry, burn off some energy: go for a walk, jog or run!

STOP! PRESS PAUSE

So, now you know what anger feels like when it's building up inside your body – but what do you do when you recognize that feeling?

First, do nothing.

Yep, that's right. Not a single thing.

When you act without thinking, you put your impulsive inferno brain in charge.[4] That's why it's important to give yourself some time to think before you do anything and ask yourself the following questions.

- **What are some of the different ways I could respond to this situation?**
- **What could help right now?**
- **Am I about to act impulsively or have I thought things through?**
- **What will the consequences of my actions be?**

INNER HERO

Count to five slowly and breathe deeply next time you're angry. Repeat until you're calm.

---

[4] Remember how I said you have a choice about which part of your brain to listen to when you get angry? Well, if you don't use your smart brain to control your fire power, your impulsive brain can make you do things that end up being bad for you. Sort of like hitting a punching bag so hard that it rocks away from you . . . then comes back and hits you in the face.

In the heat of an angry moment giving in to your impulsive brain might seem like a good idea. But it's likely that you'll feel very bad about it afterwards. Acting before you think can be dangerous! It can harm both you and others, as it can lead you to make decisions that don't consider other people's feelings or physical well-being – two things that superheroes have to keep in mind at all times.

Knowing how to calm yourself down when you feel angry is a true superhero skill. There are a few ways that you might do this.

YOU COULD TRY GOING INTO A DIFFERENT ROOM OR GOING OUTSIDE.

Sometimes fresh air cools you down physically as well as mentally!

YOU COULD TAKE SOME DEEP BREATHS.

It's important to breathe (obviously!), but breathing slowly and deeply really does help you calm down. This is because it gets more oxygen into your lungs and switches on the part of your brain that makes you calmer.

Once you have taken time to stop and think, you will be in a much better space to decide how to act. If you were angry at someone else, you might want to explain to them what you were upset about. It's much easier to explain this sort of thing when you have taken a **moment to press pause**.

Even after the angry feelings have gone away, you may still feel annoyed and cross about whatever started it. You might feel as though you have things you want to say and people you want to say them to. That's perfectly normal. Often we are upset about things that we have every right to be upset about, and in these instances it's especially important to explain our feelings to others. **Waiting until you feel calmer** can help you say these things in a clearer way.

Take a moment to think about the last time you heard someone shouting. Can you remember what they actually said? Probably not, right? If you want to be heard, it's important to stay calm when you are expressing yourself. That way, people are more likely to listen to what you are saying, and to respond in the way that you would like them to. Shouting at another person usually just makes them feel defensive. They stop listening to what you are

saying, and instead start thinking about what they are going to say in response. Every superhero needs to master the skill of talking calmly – after all, if you let your anger get the better of you, then what's the difference between you and a villain?

INNER HERO

List three things that calm you down when you're angry. Tell your family and friends what those are!

Certain things can make it more likely that you will feel angry, like being tired or hungry.[5] Knowing what these things are can **help you to plan ahead**. For example, you can make it less likely you'll get really angry by something as simple as having healthy snacks on hand and by getting enough sleep.

---

[5] My dad once yelled at a street lamp for ten minutes when he bumped into it because he hadn't eaten anything all day.

HARNESS THE HEAT

When you learn to control your fire power, you can use it to do some **amazing things**. Fires start for a reason. If you didn't care about something, you wouldn't get angry in the first place. Sometimes, we feel anger because we are passionate about something – and, in this way, anger can actually help us to learn what we really care about.

Harnessing the heat means channelling your fire power to make a **change towards something positive**. Anger has helped people to achieve some amazing things for society over the years. In the early twentieth century it drove suffragettes in Britain, the US and other parts of the world to protest and get the vote for some women. The trick, when it comes to anger, is to channel the fire power into something worthwhile.

Everyone has something that they are **passionate** about. Sometimes, you know exactly what it is straight away. Other times, you might need a bit of a nudge to find out what it is. If you're struggling to think of something you are passionate about, it can help to ask yourself the following questions.

1. WHAT AM I MOST INTERESTED IN RIGHT NOW?

Sports, celebrities, the environment - or something else!

2. IS THERE ANYTHING THAT RELATES TO THIS INTEREST WHICH I MAY FEEL ANGRY ABOUT AND WOULD LIKE TO SEE CHANGE?

For example, if you are interested in the environment, you might want to help a species that's endangered, or encourage people to use less plastic.

3. WHAT ARE MY SKILLS?

Maybe you're a confident public speaker, or are really good at organizing events. Maybe you're great at a certain sport or a particular game.

OUTER HERO

Can you use any of the answers above to think of an interesting way to raise awareness (or maybe money!) to help create positive change?

Now, think of your answers. Can you see a cool way that you could use your skills to raise awareness (or even money!) and help **create the change you want**? Perhaps you could organize a sports tournament at school and ask parents to sponsor you, with the money you raise going towards your cause? You could even write a letter to a celebrity or public figure who cares about the same thing, and ask them to talk about the issue on social media! Are there any groups or people already working towards the change you'd like to see who you could help? You could ask your parents or teacher to help you research this, if you're not sure.

Superheroes exist in all sorts of ways. You don't have to fly into a burning building to make a big change. You only need to see what you're good at, and know how to use your fire power to help you achieve the things you believe in.

You have a choice about what kind of superhero you will be. Anger can be powerful, and only truly powerful people are able to control their fire power to **put it to good use**. You can either use your fire power to make a positive change, or you can let it control you. The choice is yours.

FIGHTING FIRE
WITH FIRE

Other people get angry too, and at times you will be with others who are experiencing their own bursts of impulsive anger. When you do, remember that not everyone is training to be a superhero like you.

Think of a time when someone got angry with you – maybe it was your parent, a sibling or a friend. What made them angry? How could you tell? How did they behave? Maybe they yelled, left the room, or just stayed silent.

How did you respond to their anger? Did you remain calm? Was there anything that you could have done differently.[6]

Next time that someone around you becomes angry, here are a few things you can keep in mind to help you handle the situation.

[6] If you've already got your telepathy superpower, all this should be a piece of cake. If not, don't worry – you'll get to that chapter soon!

INNER HERO

If you get angry can you safely say you want time to think? If yes, walk away, think, then talk about it later!

LISTEN.

They might just want to rant about whatever is making them angry. If that's the case, listening may be all it takes for them to calm down.

STAY CALM.

Anger can be infectious! Keep your smart brain engaged, so that if you do say anything it will be exactly what you want to say.

YOU DON'T HAVE TO AGREE!

Listening to someone is not the same as agreeing with them.

YOU DON'T HAVE TO FIND THE ANSWER.

It can be easy to feel as though you should solve the problem at hand. In most cases, though, the other person won't expect you to have all the answers.

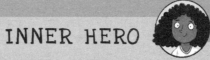
TRY TO UNDERSTAND THE OTHER PERSON'S POINT OF VIEW BEFORE YOU RESPOND.

No one wants to be told 'I understand' by someone who really doesn't get it!

It's also important to remember that another person's anger is not your fault, or your responsibility. It is their emotion, not yours. You can't control what sparks other people's fire power; **all you can do is manage your own**.

TAKE CARE OF YOURSELF

Above all, stay safe! Most people don't become aggressive when they are angry, but if you do think another person is so angry that they might hurt you, then you need to get away from them. Maybe they're making threats to hurt you or someone else, or have thrown things around and broken objects. These can be warning signs that things aren't safe.

This anger doesn't have to be directed at you physically; it's possible for you to feel hurt emotionally too. This is not OK. Go somewhere safe.

As soon as you can, find a grown-up you trust (such as a parent, caregiver or teacher) and tell them what is happening. Explain that you need help, and that you are worried you might get hurt. Even superheroes need help sometimes, and **no one has the right to hurt or threaten you**.

There are other places you can get help too, such as phoning Childline to talk to someone about what's happening or the police if you don't feel safe.[7]

---

[7] Check out the list on page 181 for other places you can find help.

'I've got a maths test on Friday I have to study for . . . and football practice two nights this week . . . and Dad said I need to clean my room . . . and what did my friend mean when she said that thing earlier?'

Sound familiar?

Do you ever feel as though your head is completely full of thoughts like this?

If you do, you're not alone! There are so many things always competing for our attention that it's hardly surprising we can feel **overwhelmed** a lot of the time.

However, as any good superhero will tell you, if you want to achieve anything, **you need to keep a clear head**. All you need are the right tools. This chapter is all about seeing, smelling, feeling, tasting and hearing things in a different way. In other words, you're about to discover how to enhance all of your senses to superhero levels. Cool!

INNER HERO

Experiment with your bedroom. Do you feel calmer if it's tidy rather than messy? Maybe you're happier when there's a colourful poster on the wall?

When your head is buzzing, you might try to quieten the noise by distracting yourself. For example, you might watch TV or read a book. But even then, you can still have things running through your mind. Maybe instead of watching telly you're worrying you should be preparing for your next football tournament or dance competition – but how are you supposed to focus on anything with that racket in your head?

Enter your new superpower: **enhanced senses**.

Once you've developed this power, you should find it a little easier to dial down the noise, concentrate on what matters and actually relax.

Sounds good, right?

To really be able to do this in any situation – be it in a stressful exam or just lying in bed staring at the ceiling – you need to **focus on the right now**. Not what happened last week or this morning. Not what might be going to happen in the future. What is happening now, in the present moment, in your mind, body and surroundings.

When you are able to do this, **you worry less about all the other distracting stuff**. You can do this by using your enhanced senses to concentrate on what you are seeing, hearing, smelling and feeling in any given moment.

Learning to take notice of yourself and the things around you takes some practice, especially in stressful situations, but you'll be grateful for it when you're able to stay calm, even as an alien horde invades Earth![1] But before you get to that level, you first need to learn to relax when you're just sitting at home.

---

[1] Trust me. When you are being chased by an alien horde, you want to be thinking about how to avoid that low-hanging tree branch – not the joke that your friends didn't laugh at earlier in the day.

OBSERVING YOUR BODY

For many people, bedtime is the time of day when their head becomes the most full of thoughts – just when they need it not to be! Often, lying in bed is the first chance they've had all day to think about the things that have happened to them. The only problem is that a noisy head doesn't usually lead to a very good night's sleep.

Sleep is important. It's your body's main opportunity to repair and regenerate. It's the time when your brain gets to process memories and new things you've learned. Sleeping even keeps your immune system healthy, so you're less likely to get sick.[2]

INNER HERO

Before sleeping practise tensing up your muscles so you're stiff like raw spaghetti, then relax like you've been cooked.

When you start using your enhanced senses, bedtime can become something really positive. It can be a lovely moment of quiet and calm. Lying in bed, relaxed and ready to fall asleep, is a great time to focus on your body – and it's also the perfect opportunity to **practise your new superpower**.

---

[2] Your immune system is sort of like a coat of armour that has the power to heal you – plus it's basically invisible and super tiny, which makes it even more awesome.

Here's a story about Jo.[3] Jo was having a hard time at school, and was worried a lot – about fitting in, about not fitting in, about not wearing the right clothes. Things were worse at night, as Jo had more time to concentrate on all these worries when alone in bed. Then Jo read a book that explained a cool new way to focus on your breathing, a trick that would help to tune out bedtime worries and noise. The book described how to breathe in deeply by imagining a balloon in your tummy filling up with air. When you breathe out, the book said, you should imagine blowing all the air out of the balloon. So, Jo started practising this every night in bed. Soon, Jo found it much easier to switch off the thoughts and worries – and, as a result, slept much better!

---

[3] I can neither confirm nor deny whether Jo is me. As you know, a superhero must protect their secret identity!

Learning to focus on your breath is a great skill. It is just one of the many ways you can bring your attention to your body, and you can do it any time you feel worried or stressed – it doesn't have to just be at bedtime. It might seem too simple to be true, but concentrating very closely on your breath really does help to make all the other thoughts in your head quieter. In fact, breathing deeply sends more oxygen to your brain, and also lets your brain cells know that things like your heart rate need to slow down.

Now it's your turn! Start by imagining that balloon in your belly. Then, once you are really focused on your breath, have a go at moving all of your attention to just one of your senses. For example, concentrate on what you can hear, and try to really focus on the individual sounds. Don't worry if you find this difficult or if you can't concentrate for very long. This is something that takes time to master!

Here are some suggestions to help you really focus on each of your five senses.

HEARING:

Listen to some music without doing anything else. Can you figure out what the different instruments are?

SIGHT:

Pick a colour, then see how many objects you can find in your room which are that colour.

TOUCH:

What parts of your body are currently touching something? Focus on the areas where you can feel more pressure, like your feet on the floor. Do you feel warm or cold? Is it hard or soft? Stroking a pet is another good way to focus on the sensation of touch.

SMELL:

Go into the kitchen when someone in your house is cooking. Close your eyes and see if you can identify the different smells around you.

TASTE:

Even if you are not eating, your mouth will be full of tastes – maybe even your last snack! Run your tongue along your teeth and gums. Can you taste anything?

OUTER HERO

Take a minute to list all of the things you can hear when people stop talking. Maybe do this with your family or friends and compare what you heard!

BRINGING THE INSIDE OUT

It can be tough to find the words to describe how you are feeling. In the English language, at least, we seem to have pretty limited options when it comes to talking about how we feel and why.[4] That's probably why people create their own words, like 'meh' or 'urgh'. It could also be why people love using emojis so much – those little pictures portray a wide range of emotions that words don't always cover.

Which emoji do you most feel like today?

It can be more than one. Some days, you might feel like a whole lot of different emojis all at the same time – and that's perfectly OK.

Sometimes, it's a bit tricky to tell the difference between your emotions, but you can learn how to do it with just a bit of practice. If you've already read the chapter about your telepathy superpower, then you'll know all about working out how others are feeling. Well, much like with telepathy, when it comes to

---

[4] If you know another language that has better words for feelings, let me know. I might fly around the world a lot, but I'm bad at learning languages. I mainly communicate through hand gestures and the occasional dance battle.

working out how you are feeling, you need to learn to **recognize the clues in your own body**.

Take a moment right now to think about a recent time when you **felt happy**, when you were really enjoying or looking forward to something. It could be five minutes ago, a day ago or even longer. What did it feel like? What was happening in your body? How were you behaving? How do you think you looked to other people? Your answers might include some of the following things.

- **I was smiling more.**
- **I was laughing.**
- **I had more energy.**

When you pay attention to what you're feeling in this way, you're not only noticing what's happening on the inside but also the things on the outside that show your emotions. You're using your **enhanced senses** to understand how your body works, and how your feelings might look to others. What's more, doing this can help you to identify other people's feelings too!

OUTER HERO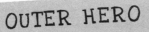

Develop someone else's enhanced senses by switching something around in a room and then make them guess what's different!

Smiling, laughing and feeling energetic are all positive reactions to feelings, and it's possible to sense and see negative emotions too. Sadness may bring a heavy feeling to your belly, tears to your eyes and a wave of tiredness. Your body might feel a bit heavier, and it might seem to take more effort to do things you usually do easily.

Of course, happy and sad are just two opposite ends of a scale. Here's where emojis are helpful again! They show that there are many other emotions between happy and sad. Part of being your best superhero self is learning to notice which emotions you're feeling, and understanding that every single one is OK. When you really master your enhanced senses, it becomes clear that it's totally normal to feel happy, sad, angry and everything in between at some point . . . and sometimes all at once!

It's not your feelings themselves that make the difference, but **how you respond to them**.

LISTEN, FEEL AND FEED EMOTIONS

We can't always stop bad things that upset us from happening. However, we can allow ourselves to simply feel our feelings, all the while knowing that the feelings won't last forever. Experiencing our feelings in this way can help us to learn and to grow.

Here's a story about Samia. On the weekend, Samia was planning to go ice-skating for the first time ever. She had always loved watching videos of ice-skaters, and couldn't wait to try it out. But, the night before she was due to go, a twig got trapped under the front wheel of her bike while she was riding it, and she fell and hurt her arm.

'No ice-skating for you, I'm afraid,' her dad said.

Samia knew her dad was right, of course. She knew it wouldn't be safe to go ice-skating with an injured arm, but that didn't stop her from feeling sad and disappointed. So, tears pricking her eyes, Samia ran upstairs to her room.

INNER HERO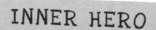

If you feel sad, try saying to yourself, 'I can handle this feeling, I am strong and in control'.

There are two ways Samia's story could have unfolded from here.

1. SHE COULD HAVE GIVEN IN TO THE TEARS AND HIDDEN UNDER THE BEDCOVERS.

In this version, Samia didn't want to feel sad, but she didn't know how to stop it, so she focused on her feelings of disappointment and fed the thoughts that she was missing out. Since it was getting late, Samia decided that maybe it was best to just stay alone in her room.

2. OR, SHE COULD HAVE STAYED UPSTAIRS IN HER ROOM FOR LONG ENOUGH TO REALIZE THAT, EVEN THOUGH SHE FELT SAD, OVERTHINKING THINGS WOULD ONLY MAKE THE FEELING BIGGER.

She reminded herself that the feelings of disappointment wouldn't last forever. Then, Samia put some music on. She closed her eyes and focused on what she could hear. It was her favourite band, and soon she felt herself enjoying the sounds. Samia's attention shifted to her arm. It would heal eventually, and Samia knew there would be other chances to go skating in the future. She also knew that being around her family would cheer her up, so she left her room and went downstairs. Since she had to stay home and rest anyway, she might as well make the most of it and spend time with them.

Which of these endings do you think would be the most useful to Samia in this situation? It's number two, right? In the second ending, Samia listened to her feelings by engaging her enhanced senses to accept them and move on. In the first ending, however, Samia let her feelings take control – and just ended up lonelier and unhappier.

It's not possible to stop sadness or tough times from happening. **They are a normal part of life.** Sometimes, they can actually help us to appreciate and enjoy happier times even more. However, you don't have to let sadness or tough times control you. When you learn how to help yourself move through sad feelings to come out the other side feeling better, you'll also learn how to help others do the same. This is a **two-for-the-price-of-one** kind of superpower!

Here are some things you can try next time you feel down about something.

- **Focus on one sense and use the breathing technique from page 55 to make your head less busy.**
- **Eat a nice meal, take a shower or go outside and get some fresh air. Looking after your body can help to lift your mood.**
- **Make a playlist of feel-good music to listen to when you are feeling a bit down.**
- **Try turning your situation around. Is there anything you can do now that you couldn't before you felt sad?**

If you find yourself feeling really sad and this feeling lasts for a long time it's important to talk to someone about it. You might need a bit of help to fight back against your low mood.[5]

---

[5] There are some useful places you can find help for this in the list on page 181.

SENSES JUST MAKE SENSE

Now that you've learned all about your enhanced senses superpower, it's time to turn your attention to the outside world. Not only do your senses help you to tap into your own feelings, but they also help you to feel even more **connected with the world** around you. When you are using your enhanced senses, you can start to become aware of things you might never have noticed before.

You can have a go at doing this right now!

INNER HERO

On your walk or drive to school, can you spot at least three different things you've never paid attention to before?

Take a moment to pay close attention to what's going on around you in this very instant. Think of your five senses – sight, smell, taste, hearing and touch. Now, as you focus on each sense, you might start to notice things you haven't noticed before. What are they? They can be big or small. Perhaps there's a building you walk past to get to school every day, but you haven't ever really seen it until now. Maybe you're sitting on the carpet, but you've never actually paid attention to the way it feels underneath you or when it touches your skin.

When you don't use your enhanced senses, you can miss so much! I bet there's a bunch of things you'd never noticed until you concentrated on them.

SHAPE-SHIFTING

Shape-shifters are mythical beings who are able to change their body and appearance at will. Being able to shape-shift is a pretty cool superpower! Once you learn how to do it, you can basically become anything you want to be, whenever you want.

Don't worry, I'm not expecting you to become a vampire or anything too supernatural – unless you want to, that is! What you'll be learning in this chapter is how to use your shape-shifting superpower to be flexible and open to change. However, this isn't the bend-yourself-in-half type of flexible that you get when you practise yoga (although that can be fun too). This kind of flexibility is all about your brain.

Stretch your brain for a change!

GO WITH THE FLOW

People who haven't engaged their shape-shifting superpower are often very inflexible. They struggle with change, and like to have quite strict routines. Once someone becomes a shape-shifter, though, this can change a bit. Compare the following two situations.

SCENARIO 1:

Your parents wake you up at 7 a.m., then you get in the shower. When you go into the kitchen, you reach for your favourite red bowl with matching red spoon. You wash your breakfast down with a glass of orange juice. At exactly 8.15 a.m., you leave the house and your parents drive you to your classmate's house. You arrive there ten minutes later, and you and your friend walk to school together at 8.30 a.m.

SCENARIO 2:

Your alarm goes off at 7 a.m., but you press snooze a couple of times because this morning you feel a bit sleepy. After showering, you fancy some toast, but when you get to the kitchen you find there's no bread left. That's OK – you have porridge instead. It's a nice day, so you decide to ride your bike to school and enjoy the sunshine, instead of getting dropped off in the car.

Can you tell which scenario shows some shape-shifting skills?

You got it: number two is far more flexible! In the second scenario, you don't let unexpected things – like the bread running out – upset you or set you off course. You just **adapt**, and go with another option. You leave yourself open to things you might have missed if you were too focused on following a specific schedule, such as riding your bike in the sunshine.

A routine can be useful. Knowing what to expect and when can help us to feel calm. However, if we can learn how to adapt to our mood and our environment, it opens up so many more options – options that, if we stick to a too-rigid schedule, we might otherwise miss out on.

INNER HERO

Change the order of your everyday routine for a few days at a time and find one you feel improves your day.

BE A COW!

It's normal to feel disappointed if something you were expecting doesn't happen, because things don't go to plan. Imagine you're looking forward to going to a friend's house at the weekend – but then they phone and cancel your plans. What would you do? It would be pretty easy to stay at home and sulk because your plans are ruined, right?

Perhaps you find it difficult to not feel sad or upset in situations like this, when your plans don't happen. At times like this, it can seem as though you can't help feeling down, but it's important to remember that **some things are still in your control**. It's the perfect time to shape-shift into a . . . COW! (OK, that might not make sense yet, but just keep reading!)

Even when something unplanned or unexpected happens, you have a choice about how you react to it. If you are feeling upset because of something not going how you wanted it to, there are three main things to consider.

1. CHOICE.

Ask yourself, 'Do I have to do this?' Are you choosing to stay home if plans are cancelled?

2. OPTIONS.

Ask yourself, 'What else is possible?' Could you meet another friend instead?

3. WEIGH THINGS UP.

Consider the pros and cons (good and bad things) of your options

And that's how you shape-shift into a COW! Cool, huh?

When you have considered these three things, you'll be better prepared to respond to the situation.

Working out whether you have a choice first is incredibly important. You can think of choice like this: you might be able to decide what colour vest you wear, what you have in your sandwich at lunchtime, or what breakfast cereal you eat, but you can't change the time that school starts or other people's choices. Realizing what you can and can't change tells you which things you do and don't have a choice about. This is the first step to working out which areas of your life you have the most control over.

Once you know whether you have a choice about something or not, it will be easier to know how to deal with it emotionally and physically. If you can't change it, is it better to simply accept it, and move on to something that you do have more choice about? For example, you might have planned to see a film with a friend, but your friend got sick on the day you were meant to go. You can't change the fact that your friend is sick, and you can't make them go to the film with you, so you're better not to worry about these – they're out of your control. Instead, you can consider your options. You could go to the film yourself, or you could invite another friend to go with you.

The final step is to weigh up all the pros and cons – or the **good and bad aspects** – of your situation and the options available to you. When you do this, you may even realize that a **better option** was there all along! For example, in the scenario where your friend can't go to the film with you, perhaps it has turned out to be a beautiful day. In that case, you might have more fun going to the park to enjoy the warmth and fresh air than you would have being stuck sitting in a stuffy old cinema anyway!

It can be helpful to think of your brain having a **sliding scale** from rigid (never changing your mind) to flexible (being open to changing your mind). As your shape-shifting superpower grows, you'll start to notice that you are more able to move from one end to the other when you need to.

Where do you think you are on this scale at the moment?

Rigid thinker
Likes things to be the same
Hates change

Flexible thinker
Finds change easier to handle
Enjoys the challenge of new things

0 1 2 3 4 5 6 7 8 9 10

When you start shape-shifting into a COW more often, you might feel your thinking style start to change. You'll probably notice yourself moving more often towards the flexible end of the scale. If you want to see the effects of learning to shape-shift, you could rate yourself on this scale again later, after you've started putting your new superpower into action!

INNER HERO

Try picking something new when you go to the supermarket or a restaurant. You might still prefer your original choice, but you'll never know if you don't try . . .

CAN YOU BE ANYTHING?

Being an agile shape-shifter means being able to **think flexibly**. This relies heavily on imagination and on being able to come up with alternative solutions to problems. Imagine, for instance, you are fighting a monster who suddenly reveals it has wings and flies off. Do you carry on waving your sword in the air, or do you pick up a bow and arrow?[1]

Shape-shifting is all about being flexible and opening your mind to new possibilities and new ways of learning. The desire to think beyond what you can do now and imagine what you might do in the future is a

shape-shifting master stroke! **Believing that something might be possible** is the first step to doing it. You can think of this as a bit like when someone learns to ride a bike. They might start using training wheels to help them balance, and can't imagine ever riding without them. Then, they might see some older kids riding bikes without training wheels in the park, and that motivates them to give it a go.

---

[1] This really happened to me once. I spent about half an hour jumping in the air, trying to grab the monster's leg.

Trying new things can be scary at first, but also very exciting. We each have our own personal preferences, from what we eat for lunch to what we watch on TV. However, it can be worth trying new things, even if you really love your favourite things. After all, if you never try anything new, you might never realize all the things you could be missing out on that are even better!

There are loads of ways you can use shape-shifting to make your daily life a bit more exciting when a small obstacle pops up. Here are just a few examples.

IF YOUR USUAL JOURNEY TO SCHOOL ISN'T POSSIBLE,

you could take a different route. Maybe you'll find a new route that's even quicker?

IF YOUR FAVOURITE RESTAURANT RUNS OUT OF YOUR USUAL ORDER,

try something new. Maybe it will become your new favourite dish?

IF YOU CAN'T PLAY IN THE PLAYGROUND AT BREAK OR LUNCHTIME,

play an indoor game instead. You might discover a fun new game!

By being a flexible thinker, you can come up with **new ideas to adapt to unexpected situations** like the ones above. When it comes to your everyday life, shape-shifting is an incredibly useful superpower!

Learning how to shape-shift might feel impossible when you start out, but it's actually easier than you may think. Try this activity to stretch your brain and develop your new superpower. First, choose a boring object like a cup or pencil – anything you want. List all the things that object can be used for, apart from its obvious use. This is a good way to push yourself out of your comfort zone and encourage your brain to think in new ways.

When you do this activity, it might feel as though you're trying to shape-shift a random object into something else, but what you're actually doing is forcing yourself to look past what you're told that object is for. You are imagining all of the other things that object could be. Have you ever heard the saying **'think outside the box'**? That's basically what you are doing!

This is a great example of being a flexible – and also a creative! – thinker. Having the ability to think like this will help you to both problem-solve and adapt to difficult situations, because you will be able to shape-shift your thoughts and actions in order to learn and grow.

OUTER HERO

Can you use your flexible thinking to find a use for something your family normally throws away? For example, used coffee grounds can make a great fertilizer for plants or old toothbrushes can be used to clean jewellery.

RULES RULE

You may have already realized that life is full of all sorts of **different rules**. We have to know and understand what many of those rules are in order to live our life every day – like a red traffic light means stop, and a queue at a shop till means we have to wait. Lots of these rules are unspoken – they are learned from being in the world and watching what others do. Not knowing these rules can be really tricky – you can find yourself doing the wrong thing without even knowing it!

Every single one of us – child or adult – is trying to learn these rules all the time. The **good thing** is that you are always learning. The **bad thing** is that you're always learning!

Rules can vary in different places, which means the way you act sometimes needs to shape-shift. For instance, would you act the same way in the cinema as you would watching football? It might be fine to shout and cheer at the players in a football game, but yelling at the film probably wouldn't go down very well with everyone else in the cinema!

Rules can rule! They can really help to guide us and keep people happy and safe. But sometimes rules can be quite controlling in a negative way and can limit the choices we have, for example who we can marry or what we can wear. Working out which rules help and which harm can be tricky. But knowing what the rules are in the first place is the best place to start – then you can try to understand why these rules have been put in place.

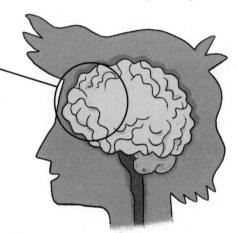

The frontal lobe: the clever bit of your brain that helps you learn how to act in different situations

HERE'S A COOL FACT:

Your brain is actually wired to work out a lot of these rules automatically! The part of your brain that helps you to learn the rules for how to act in different situations sits just behind your forehead. This part of your brain develops at a different rate in each person and is actually still growing and learning until you are in your mid-twenties, so it can take a lot of practice to up your shape-shifting game. It's definitely worth it, though!

You might think hyper intelligence is all about being born smart and having a natural advantage over others, but it's not. What this superpower is really about is **patience**, **time** and **determination**. In this chapter, you're going to learn how to become a mastermind in any situation. As well as covering planning, problem-solving and creating new (and useful) habits, you'll learn how to really use your brain in any given situation.[1]

When I put it all in a list like that it sounds a bit boring, but I promise it isn't! Do Iron Man or Shuri ever seem boring or lame to you? Nope! Tony Stark is one of the most intelligent Avengers, and everyone thinks he's hilarious. Shuri is the smartest human in the world, but she has loads of fun with Black Panther. These two are superheroes because they've mastered one of the most powerful weapons of all: **their brains**.

---

[1] A necessary skill for any superhero: if you have twenty seconds to save five people, you have to be able to figure out how to save them. Being strong and fast is great, but neither will be much help if you don't have a strategy! Trust me, I learned this one the hard way . . .

HYPER-HEALTHY HABITS

If you've already read the chapter about controlling your fire power, then you know that the front part of your brain (your smart brain) is the bit that helps you to think before you act. Scientists actually know quite a lot about this as a result of a railway worker who damaged the front of his brain in an accident. After this unfortunate injury, his personality changed and he had difficulty with planning and making decisions. This showed scientists just how important the damaged section of his brain was for developing those skills.

What's more, the front part of your brain is also the last part to fully develop. Some experts say your **smart brain** isn't fully developed until your mid-twenties. What this means is that learning to be organized and make decisions can require extra practice when you are still young.

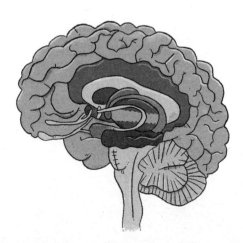

Each new day brings a whole set of new challenges that you can use to develop your **hyper intelligence**. All you need to do is start creating some **healthy habits**! A huge part of this is planning. If your life isn't organized, it can feel like a whirlwind. In the morning, for example, you might find yourself losing things, forgetting what you need to pack[2] and rushing around, and that just gets your day off to a bad start.

INNER HERO

Write out a plan (or keep a diary!) for the following week, including any fun activities you may have planned.

Happily, there are some really easy ways to use your hyper intelligence to get organized and plan ahead. By doing this, you will ensure you always know what's happening and how to handle it. Your days will feel much smoother, and you won't feel so rushed. Here are a few suggestions to start putting your new superpower into action.

HAVE A CHECKLIST OF THINGS YOU NEED TO DO EACH NIGHT BEFORE BED.

It might include, for example, checking that your school bag is packed and ready, and that your clothes for the next day are clean.

[2] Once, I forgot to wear my mask and only realized when I was already standing there in front of the baddie, with my face in full view. Luckily, that particular villain's locked away now, otherwise it could have been a bit of a problem . . .

FILL A BOX WITH EVERYTHING YOU NEED TO DO YOUR HOMEWORK –

things like pens, paper, pencils and sharpeners, and any other stationery. Having everything in one place will save you a surprising amount of time when it comes to doing your homework.

KEEP YOUR ROOM TIDY.

Tidy room, tidy mind! Having a clean and organized space will save you time by making it easier to find the things you need.

CLEAR OUT THE CLUTTER.

Sort out any clothes, books and toys you no longer want or use, then sell them or give them away. Not only will you have less stuff around to distract you, but you will also get the satisfaction of helping others!

If you do these things often enough, they will soon become healthy habits (also known as your superhero instinct!). They might feel hard to do at first, but if you stick with them, being organized will soon be so routine you won't even have to think about it.

Habits take time to form, and that's why it's important to keep them up. The first time that you do something, your brain starts to make new connections. Then, the more you do that same thing, the stronger those connections become. It's when you do something over and over again that it eventually becomes a habit.

As you develop your hyper intelligence by becoming more organized, you'll find it's helpful when others make an effort to do the same. Think about your family at home. Do you share out the household chores, or does one person do most of the work? If you take the time as a family to set up a rota and give each person certain jobs, it will make it easier to get everything done. What's more, it will also mean that everyone has a role to play in the home, which can give you a sense of responsibility and importance. You could even make the boring tasks more fun by turning them into a friendly competition.[3] Finishing a task all by yourself can feel really good – especially if you do it before anyone else has finished theirs!

OUTER HERO

Volunteer to take on responsibility for a chore around the house, such as watering plants or washing the dishes on certain nights of the week.

[3] I use my hyper intelligence to beat my little brother at the 'how fast can you clean your room' game, by planning my tidying strategy. He thinks it's cheating . . . to which I say, I'm older, so deal with it.

CONCENTRATION
IS KEY

Concentrating can be difficult. You might be trying really hard to focus on a book that you need to read, but there's so much else going on. You can hear a song playing that you like, you remember something you forgot to tell your friend earlier and want to message them about it now, and you get sidetracked thinking about your plans for the weekend.

In instances like this, all you need to know how to do is unlock your maximum concentration capacity. It sounds complicated, but really it's as easy as ABC!

ANTICIPATE.

In other words, prepare and think ahead. Ask yourself: 'What do I need to do to complete this task?' Write it all down! Then, break it up into different steps and complete one step at a time. Think about what needs to be completed first, and try not to put off harder work until later. Most people can concentrate for only twenty minutes at the most, so make sure you take breaks.

BUCKLE DOWN.

Stay determined and stick to the job. For example, if you are doing your homework, try to find a quiet place where you won't be disturbed and pick a regular time to do it. You could choose to do it right after school, so that you will have time for yourself in the evening - having something to look forward to can help you stay focused. If you get too distracted at home, perhaps there's a homework club at your school or you could go to your local library?

INNER HERO

Make a list of all the things you're looking forward to — it helps to keep you motivated!

COLLABORATE AND COMPLETE.

Collaborate means to work with others. If you need help, ask for it. Keeping quiet when you are finding things difficult often only makes it even harder to finish! Sometimes, you just need a point in the right direction, and you'll soon find the answers for yourself. Get a parent to look over your work, or check with a teacher if you don't understand something. If you struggle with one subject in particular, maybe you could work with a friend? They might find some things hard that you find easier, so you could help each other out.

• •

Like all healthy habits, learning to concentrate will take some time and practice before it starts to feel normal.

There are lots of ways to get better at planning and concentration outside of just your schoolwork. Why not try something fun like learning a new skill? For instance, you could choose a recipe to try cooking, and set a date to make it for your family. You'll need to write a shopping list of ingredients and plan a trip to the supermarket. Most recipes have quite a few steps, so you'll also need to weigh and prepare your ingredients. And don't forget the third step above – **collaborate, and get some help when you need it**!

BIG PROBLEMS, BIGGER BRAIN

Much like your muscles, you can **exercise your brain to make it stronger** – but you also need to keep exercising it in new and different ways to stop it from getting bored!

Getting stuck while you are trying to solve a problem can actually be a good thing. If you take time to find a solution, you are more likely to remember what you have learned in the process. When it comes to figuring things out, if you always stick to an easy option that you know will work, you can miss out on opportunities to learn. Doing things the easy way doesn't exercise your brain.

The next time you tackle a new problem, try asking yourself the following questions.

- **Do I understand what I am meant to do?**
- **What do I already know about this?**
- **What do I need to find out?**
- **How can I test out if my solution is the right one?**

INNER HERO

Try out a new activity that involves strategy and problem solving, like chess or coding.

You might not get everything right the first time round. That's OK! You should still have a go, even if you might be wrong.

As Albert Einstein said, 'A person who never made a mistake never tried anything new.'[4] It's important to know that it's **OK to be wrong**. It's better to try something and learn that it doesn't work than it is to never try in the first place. Just knowing this can give you the confidence to try a new approach.

As if trying to solve problems isn't already hard enough, most people can remember only seven bits of information at any one time.[5] (This is why long phone numbers or lists of objects can be tricky to remember.) Having such limited knowledge can make finding the solution to a problem even more difficult, but the cool thing is that you can strengthen part of your brain to improve your memory! There's a seahorse-shaped bit of your brain that sits behind your ear. This is called the **hippocampus**, and it is the part involved in **storing memories** – and, with practice, you can actually make it bigger! Here are a few tricks to get you started.

---

[4] Can you really argue with Einstein? He's one of the most well-known geniuses to ever exist!

[5] At the moment, I can remember what I want for breakfast, what I want for lunch, what I want for dinner, what I want for a snack, what I'd name my dog if my parents let me get one, how I'd defeat Thanos if I was in the Avengers, and how many times I've been to the loo today. Probably not much of that is very useful for problem-solving, though . . .

TRY GROUPING INFORMATION INTO CHUNKS.

For example, on a shopping list, you could remember yoghurt, milk and butter as 'dairy'. If you are trying to remember a phone number, you could group it up into sets of three or four digits like this: 123-4567-8910.

A MNEMONIC IS A PATTERN OF WORDS, LETTERS OR IDEAS THAT HELPS YOU TO REMEMBER CERTAIN INFORMATION MORE EASILY.

You may already know the mnemonic ROY G BIV for the colours of the rainbow (Red, Orange, Yellow, Green, Blue, Indigo and Violet).

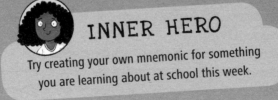

INNER HERO

Try creating your own mnemonic for something you are learning about at school this week.

PLAY GAMES THAT PUT
YOUR MEMORY TO TEST!

For example, spot the difference or a memory card game, or read a story then retell it to a friend in your own words.

DID YOU KNOW THAT YOUR MOOD
AFFECTS WHAT YOU REMEMBER?

When you feel happy and relaxed, it is easier to form stronger memories. A clever part of your brain called the amygdala stores these kinds of memories which are linked to your emotions at the time. Experiment with things that help you to feel relaxed when you are trying to concentrate – perhaps quiet music playing, or having some of your favourite things around you.

When you develop your hyper intelligence by taking the time to clear away any clutter and make life more organized, you'll soon notice how much easier you find it to **focus on the things you want and need to do**. Add in your new tricks for concentrating, and you'll also be less likely to give in to distraction. You'll be uber-focused and reaching Shuri levels of brain power in no time at all!

INNER HERO

Create a new game with your own rules to test out on your family and friends, maybe even your classmates!

Superheroes are known for being pretty strong. Even the heroes who are human are stronger than your average person. Just look at Black Widow – she constantly kicks butt!

But what does it actually mean to be strong? Is it about having hulking[1] biceps bursting out of your T-shirt, or is there more to it? The answer is both! Keeping active and giving your body everything it needs to be healthy is always good, but **being strong is also a state of mind**. Being fit and healthy is great, but you also need a strong mind to reach your full potential. A strong mind gives you the power and determination to push harder, faster and further and be the very best you can be.

I feel healthy and strong.

---

[1] Get it? *Hulk*-ing!

In this chapter, you're going to learn all about gaining super strength in both your body and your mind. I'll give you some tips on how to be a bit more active, as well as describing how you can start to shape your mind so that you feel stronger.

As you develop your super strength, you'll discover this superpower has some pretty great benefits besides simply making your body and your mind stronger. For one, you'll become more engaged with your body. You may also find that you don't get ill as often, and it may help you to avoid developing serious health problems. Your super strength can even help you to **concentrate** at school, to **sleep better** and to feel **less stressed**. And, when you walk, run or cycle instead of taking a car, train or bus, you're even doing your bit for the planet!

Possibly the best thing about super strength is that you have no limits with it! You can always get stronger by putting time into looking after your body and your mind. It is also the easiest superpower to see yourself making progress with. From week to week, you can easily see yourself **growing stronger**, **going further**, **getting faster**.

SLEEP, EAT, EXERCISE, REPEAT

Keeping your mind and your body strong can be a bit of a balancing act, because there are three main parts to staying healthy: you need to **eat well**, you need to be **active**, and you also need to make time to **relax**.

Different parts of each of these three things appeal to different people. You just have to find the right balance for you. It's important not to spend too much time and energy on just one thing, and not enough on the others. If you don't get the balance right, you will only find it harder to feel your happiest and healthiest in your mind and your body. You might fairly quickly start to feel like you're missing out on things, too.

So, let's go through everything you need to keep your mind and your body strong so that you can find exactly what works for you, shall we?

EATING WELL

Of the three things you need to do to keep healthy, eating a **balanced diet** can be the most tricky for some people. You might already eat a balanced diet, with lots of good protein and fruit and vegetables. Go, you! Keep doing what you're doing. If you don't though, you might need to consider changing your eating habits. Doing so isn't necessarily easy,[2] but it will help you in the long term. It can be helpful to imagine your body as being like an engine. In order for it to run at its best, you need to power it with the right fuel.

Here's an overview of the sorts of fuel a superhero's engine runs on.

- **Fresh fruit and vegetables are essential! They are a good source of vitamins, minerals and fibre.**
- **Carbohydrates provide you with energy, and can be found in things like pasta, potatoes, bread or rice.**
- **Protein repairs and refuels your entire body, and can be found in meat, pulses such as lentils and chickpeas, beans, eggs and nuts.**
- **Dairy also contains protein, plus vitamins and calcium, which keeps your bones strong. Yoghurt, milk and cheese are all examples of dairy products.**

---

[2] Especially if your parents buy your food, like mine do. I'm a superhero, but I'm still not allowed to buy the cereal I want. What's up with that?!

- If you don't eat animal products,[3] you can get the same nutrients that dairy provides from seeds, lentils and leafy vegetables, too.
- Fats tend to have a bit of a bad reputation, but some fats are actually healthy! Fats actually help you to absorb certain vitamins that you wouldn't be able to otherwise, so every one of us needs small amounts to keep our body healthy. Avocados and nuts are both tasty and easy sources of healthy fats. Try to avoid too many fatty processed foods such as chips, cakes and fast food which are not good for your heart or your health.
- Sugar may be found naturally, such as in fruit, or can be added to food such as cakes and fizzy drinks (refined sugar). Refined sugar doesn't contain nutrients and can actually be quite harmful to your teeth and health.

OUTER HERO

Try to make a healthy meal with your family that includes all the major food groups.

---

[3] I've met loads of people who have different diets. There are vegans (no meat, dairy or animal products), vegetarians (no meat) and pescatarians (no meat, except fish). I once even even met a dinotarian (no meat, except when they travelled back in time and hunted dinosaurs).

Here's a pie chart that shows what a healthy balance of all the main food groups looks like. The slices of the pie show how much you should be eating of each type of food. As you can see, the biggest slices are the fruit and vegetables, and carbohydrates, because this is what you should eat the most of. However, you also need to eat some protein and dairy (or dairy substitutes), as well as a small amount of healthy fats.

It can feel like a lot to have to remember all these different groups every day! An easier way to think of it is to just try to eat everything in proportion. So long as you are eating plenty of fresh, tasty vegetables, fruit and protein, it's OK to have a treat every now and then. But if you open a packet of biscuits maybe have one or two and save the rest for later!

It can actually be quite a lot of fun finding a healthy balance to your diet, especially if you get involved in choosing and preparing the food that you eat. Why not chat to whoever usually cooks your dinner about finding some healthy recipes that you can try out together?

The final thing to mention when it comes to eating well – and one of the most important things to remember – is that being strong and healthy is not about your size, your shape or your weight. Superheroes come in all sorts of unique forms. The key to being the healthiest, happiest and strongest you is feeling happy with your body and grateful for all the things it helps you to do.

KEEPING ACTIVE

Number two on the list of things to do to build your super strength is being **active**! There are actually three main parts to your physical fitness: **strength**, **flexibility** and **endurance**. Don't worry, though – you don't need to be a weightlifter, a yoga instructor and a marathon runner. Thankfully, there are other ways to do all three of these things.

Perhaps you already play a sport as part of a team? If not, you could look into joining one, or if you prefer you can also exercise alone. It's all about finding what works for you. **There is no right or wrong way to look after yourself!**

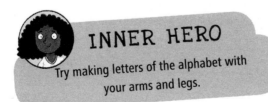

INNER HERO

Try making letters of the alphabet with your arms and legs.

Whatever your experience so far, here are a **few ideas** to get you started.

- **Go for a walk with your loved ones.**
- **Find out about sports classes or teams that you could join at your school.**
- **Try out a local running group, or go for a run with a friend.**
- **Try some stretches, or even doing yoga. You could ask an adult to help you find some videos that describe how to safely do the poses, or you could join a class.**

Of course, not everyone is able to run, jump or swim. If that's you, don't let that put you off! There are loads of activities out there for people with all sorts of abilities and experience levels.[4]

---

[4] If you've watched the Paralympic Games, you'll already know that the athletes in it are all superheroes whose bodies work in different ways. These athletes might give you some ideas of what you could be capable of! The Paralympics are part of the Olympics, and it's loads of fun to watch the events and cheer the athletes on.

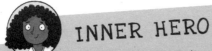

INNER HERO

Plan your time every evening to include eating a meal, doing your homework and having time to enjoy yourself.

If you need some help coming up with ideas, ask your parents or teachers to help you find the right activity for you.

Exercise and sports are great ways to release some of the body's feel-good chemicals called **endorphins,** which you'll learn about very soon. They can also give you something to aim for – with practice you will see an improvement in what you can do and see that you are stronger and more capable than you realized!

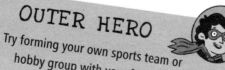

OUTER HERO

Try forming your own sports team or hobby group with your friends.

RELAXING

The third and final part of developing your super strength is learning how to **relax**. This sounds like the easiest part – and for once it is! All it means is taking time to do something that makes you **feel calm**.

Some people might relax by meditating, sitting in a quiet room, breathing deeply and letting their thoughts come and go without worrying about them. Others might prefer to take a hot bath and enjoy some music or read a book. Yet others may like to relax by doing an activity like painting or drawing. There's no right or wrong way to relax. Whatever you choose to do to relax, just make sure it's something that you do **just for you** – and not for anyone else.

Relaxing gives your mind, and your body, a rest. During this rest you can replenish your energy levels, making you feel even stronger. Like most things, the more you make time to relax, the easier it becomes, as the areas of your brain that help you do this get stronger. This means when stressful and difficult things happen in life you may find it easier to press pause and calm your body and mind.

STRONG MIND, STRONG BODY

Do you know that your brain contains millions of connections, sort of like little wires, that send messages to different parts of your body?[5] These connections use chemicals called **neurotransmitters** – if you want to be really fancy! – to send messages. These chemicals are really powerful, and they influence how you feel, from happy or excited to stressed or sad. Let's take a closer look at the main neurotransmitters: serotonin, dopamine, endorphins and adrenaline.

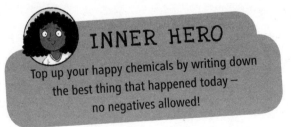

INNER HERO

Top up your happy chemicals by writing down the best thing that happened today – no negatives allowed!

---

[5] Yes, it really does! I read it in a science textbook and everything.

First up, **serotonin**. This is the one that makes you feel happy and less stressed. It is actually found all over your body, not just in your brain. There are small things that can help boost your serotonin levels, such as spending time outdoors or eating a balanced diet that includes enough carbohydrates.

Not having enough serotonin is linked to depression, which is when a person feels very sad, has no energy and doesn't enjoy things for a long period of time. People who suffer from depression often see therapists or psychologists to help them overcome it.

Dopamine is the neurotransmitter that makes you feel talkative and excited. It also plays a vital role in controlling your movements, because it works in a part of the brain that controls your balance and coordination. Dopamine can also help you to focus and concentrate. Getting a good night's sleep will keep your body's dopamine levels balanced, and listening to music has been shown to help as well!

Endorphins make you feel good, and are also your body's natural painkillers. If your endorphin levels are high, you will feel less pain and be less likely to feel stressed. Exercise, such as running, can cause a rush of endorphins.

Adrenaline is the neurotransmitter that makes you feel ready to run, be alert or even fight! This is why it's sometimes called the 'fight or flight' hormone. Adrenaline is usually released at times of stress, so it's better to reduce the levels your body produces. Practising deep breathing to stay calm can help.

Did you know that **humans are made up almost entirely of water**? And did you know that Earth is too? Pretty cool, huh! That's precisely why learning to control your water power is incredibly useful – not only are you learning to control yourself, but you're also learning how to control parts of the world around you! Who wouldn't want a superpower like that?

If you have ever spent time at the seaside, you will know that sometimes the ocean can look very still and calm, but at other times it looks full of energy and force, hitting the beach or rocks and sending water shooting into the air. Well, your worry and anxiety are a lot like the waves in the ocean: they can be so small they're barely visible, or they can be huge and terrifying, powerful enough to push you beneath the surface.

This chapter is all about **mastering your water power**. You will learn how to calm rough waters by taming your anxieties and fears, and how to harness powerful waves and channel them into tackling your worries head on.

LEARN TO SWIM

Chances are you **worry about certain things sometimes**. Perhaps it's doing a presentation in front of your whole class, or playing a sport that you hate at school. We all worry sometimes, and we worry about all sorts of things, big and small.

Even people who seem to find life easy – people like your parents or your siblings, perhaps – are more than likely to be anxious about certain things. If you feel as though you're the only one who worries about things, you could try doing a 'worry survey' in your family or with some friends. Ask them if they ever worry about things, and what they worry about. The answers might surprise you!

This is the first lesson when it comes to your water power: it is completely normal to feel worried! In fact, when you know how to overcome them, feelings of worry and anxiety can actually help you to take control of your actions. It is only when you give in to these feelings and allow them to take over that the stream becomes an uncontrollable river of worry – but managing that river is where your power kicks in!

Before you put your water power into practice, though, you need to first learn how to swim. This isn't like regular swimming, though. You need to know how to **stay afloat when the water gets rough**. So, the next time you feel yourself being swept along by a growing river of worry, you can try using these techniques to help you keep your head above the water and stay calm.

DEEP BREATHS

Slow things down! Fight fast breathing by counting to three as you breathe in, then again as you breathe out.

RELAX YOUR MUSCLES

The moment that a wave of worry hits, your muscles tense up! So, starting with your toes, squeeze and release each part of your body. Concentrate on turning your body from a dried stick of pasta to a floppy piece of cooked spaghetti.

5-4-3-2-1 SENSES

If the feeling of worry is really overwhelming you and your heart is racing, you can try focusing on your senses by listing five things you can see, four things you can touch, three things you can hear, two things you can smell, and one thing you can taste.

CALM WATERS

When feelings of worry and anxiety do take over, you can end up feeling **out of control**, and this can lead you to think in unhelpful ways. If you're being pulled along by a rushing river of worry, you're more likely to try to save yourself by jumping to conclusions and presuming that the worst is about to happen. Scared and panicked, you're less likely to take a moment to assess the situation and the options available to you, let alone pay attention to your reactions – but, of course, that's precisely what you need to do. In this manner, controlling your water power is very similar to controlling your fire power.

It can be tempting to ignore your worries altogether. Pretending something annoying doesn't exist can often seem like the easiest way to get past it, but doing this is actually really unhelpful. Not convinced? OK, then. Try this. For the next thirty seconds, think about anything you want – it can be this book, a TV show you've been watching, your favourite food or your best friend – but do not, under any circumstances, think about a pink elephant.

How did you get on?

If you're anything like me, you probably lasted all of a few seconds before your mind wandered towards that pink elephant! Well, do you know what the elephant is the same as? You guessed it: all those things you're worried about but trying your hardest to ignore.

Hey there!

If you try not to think about something, that often just leads to you thinking about it more. Dealing with worry is difficult enough as it is, but ignoring your worries can actually lead to you overthinking them, and that just makes everything seem even **bigger** and **scarier**.

When you feel worried, you can also become **stressed**. In response, your body senses this as a threat to your safety and releases adrenaline.[1] This is the point at which your worry becomes a river, and can start controlling you instead of the other way round. Swept along by the rushing water, you can panic and stop making good decisions, and get swept under by the worry.

If this happens, the best thing to do is to root yourself in certainty before you act. Don't let the torrent of water take control of you. **You need to control it.** Writing about your worries can be a good place to start. Try writing down the answers to the following questions.

---

[1] If you've already read the chapter about your fire power or about your super strength, you'll remember that adrenaline is the pesky 'fight or flight' chemical. It's what makes your heart race (and, in my case, sweat uncontrollably) when your teacher unexpectedly asks you to answer a question you definitely don't know the answer to.

- What am I worried about?
- Could this really happen?
- Does my level of fear match the situation?
- What would I say to a friend who was in the same situation?

Once you've written everything down and can see it all laid out in front of you, you'll probably find that the situation becomes a lot easier to deal with. What had started to seem like a raging river has once again become a trickling stream. What you've done here is taken a moment to think about the situation clearly, and this is the first step towards mastering your water power. **Well done!**

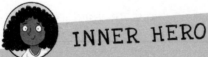

INNER HERO

Make a list of things that would stop you worrying about something you have to do. Can you make any of them happen?

LEARN TO SURF

The next step is to tackle your worry head on by making a plan to deal with it. Dealing with the worry means it's less likely to keep popping up and upsetting you, so that you can get on with your life with fewer mistakes.[2]

---

[2] I once almost forgot to teleport to Mars, because I was worrying about how my cape looked. I got there three hours late, and the Martians were really annoyed. True story.

Sometimes, just calming the water isn't enough. This is when you need to turn your worries round and use them to your **advantage**. All that adrenaline which worrying creates can actually be great for getting stuff done, because it can help you to feel stronger and to cope with change. You can think of it as being a bit like surfing – if there aren't any big waves, how are you going to do anything awesome on your surfboard? If your worry is the wave, all you need to do is learn how to stand on a surfboard and ride it!

INNER HERO

Writing a pros and cons list (see page 72) can be a good way to use the energy that worry creates to look at a situation in a different way.

The first thing to do is to **figure out a plan** for what to do when a wave of worry hits. For example, maybe you have a basketball game next week, but you haven't been able to train because of bad weather, and now you're worried that you won't be prepared for the game. Don't let that worry get in the way – use it to find another way to prepare! Perhaps you could improve your technical knowledge by watching videos of how the pros do it? You could even do something totally unrelated to sport to replenish your energy, like read a book or watch a film, so that you're ready to kick butt when the weather finally improves!

If you're feeling anxious because you're about to do something you've never done before, that can be your body's way of telling you to **do things a little differently**. It can be helpful to think of an activity you're confident doing – it might be riding a bike, or writing a poem, or baking a cake. It's probably something that you've done a lot, right? Can you remember a time you felt less confident doing it? Chances are you've practised lots to get to a place where you feel confident in what you're doing.

INNER HERO

Make two piles out of your clothes: one that makes you feel confident and one that doesn't. Now try only wearing the ones that make you feel good!

Although it's great to feel comfortable doing something familiar, that sense of **comfort can also hold you back** from trying new things because you may worry about not being as good at them at first. As a result of avoiding new things, your worry can simply grow even stronger. Realizing that a reluctance to step outside of your comfort zone is holding you back can help you to take a deep breath and face your worries head on. This can be scary, but if you do so you will soon realize just how much more you can achieve than you thought – and that is a feeling that makes the worry completely worth it!

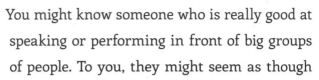

You might know someone who is really good at speaking or performing in front of big groups of people. To you, they might seem as though they were born with a natural confidence, but absolutely **everyone doubts themselves**. The only difference is that they haven't let their self-doubt and worries hold them back!

Here's a story about Bo. He stuttered when he spoke, and was worried that other people would laugh at him for it. Bo had to give presentations to his class every week, but he hated the thought of them so much that he just tried to ignore them and always ended up preparing for them at the very last minute. He'd find himself right before class frantically trying to think of something to talk about, and this only made him even more worried.

That's when Bo realized he needed to use his water power to face his worry wave and come up with a plan to surf it. First, Bo took a step back to analyse his worry. He asked himself those four questions from earlier on page 118, and came up with the following answers.

- 'I am worried that everyone will laugh at how I speak, and that no one will be interested in what I have to say.'
- 'No, there isn't any evidence that this will happen or that it's true.'
- 'I feel much more afraid of doing the presentations than I need to. And, when I don't prepare ahead of time, I only end up more scared because I put more pressure on myself.'
- 'If I had a friend in the same situation, I'd suggest they should face their worry head on and prepare for their presentations in advance, because that would give them time to practise and they would feel more prepared and confident – so that's what I'm going to do!'

By facing his worry head on and analysing it, Bo was able to come up with a plan for how to deal with it. He realized he could grab a board and **surf the wave**! He practised his presentation at home in the mirror. He repeated words and sounds that were likely to lead to a stutter. He pretended to be different characters – and he noticed that, with some accents or voices,[3] his stutter got worse, but with others it disappeared! He used these little tricks to overcome his stutter, and to develop a confident speaking voice. Now, Bo finds public speaking doesn't worry him like it did before!

---

[3] He told me some accents were from different countries, and others were from characters in films. He even did a few for me, and let's just say I was laughing so much I had to change into my backup superhero pants.

Can you think like Bo?

I know it's much easier for me to say, 'Grab a board and ride that wave!' than it is for you to actually do it – but that doesn't mean you shouldn't at least give it a try! It doesn't matter what it is that worries you – it might be public speaking like Bo, or something else altogether. All you need to remember to do is harness every wave of worry, and use it to **practise harder and get further**.

When you put your water power to use like this, you'll be surfing in no time!

REGENERATION

Sometimes in life, things might happen that are out of the ordinary and that are hard to deal with. Perhaps something happens that you don't want to happen, or perhaps someone might behave towards you in a way that you don't want them to. Whenever you face negative situations like this, it's natural to feel pain or sadness – and, sometimes, these feelings can seem to last for a long time. Maybe someone you love moves to another town, or you lose a pet you care for very much, or something big changes in your life. You might feel so down and sorry about any of these things happening that you find it difficult to see how things will ever get easier, but with time and healing, they will.

In this chapter, you're going to learn all about how sad and painful emotions show themselves, and how you can manage them when they do appear. In other words, you're going to discover your regeneration superpower! Regeneration is a hidden ability, so it's not necessarily something you control. Instead, it's something you will learn how to help happen naturally, by understanding your emotions during the healing process after something difficult.

DEALING WITH CRITICISM

Ever worked really hard on something, only to have someone turn round and tell you that you could have done better? How did it feel? If you felt a bit down because you thought the person's comment was a bad thing, that's completely normal. However, not every comment that you view as negative is always a bad thing. Take Steve Rogers, for example. Before he became Captain America, he was told he was too weak to ever be a soldier – let alone a superhero!

When you hear something about yourself that you view as negative, you'll often find yourself feeling upset. This is when strong emotions can take over and make it difficult to think clearly. So, the first thing to do if you notice this happening is to take a deep breath and slow things down.

The next thing to do is to think a bit more about the negative comment. Ask yourself, 'Is this just a mean comment, or is it actually a piece of advice that I could use to **learn** and **grow**?'[1] Are you able to use the comment to identify an area you need to

---

[1] I was once told by a rival of mine that I was bossy. Turned out everyone else thought I was a great leader, and he actually wished he was as in control as me!

work on? It helps if the person who made the comment said things in a nice way, but this doesn't always happen. Sometimes you have to look past how the comment was said in order to hear what it said, and when you do this you might find the positive in it.

Unfortunately, there are also times when someone says something that is just plain hurtful or mean. In these instances, there isn't necessarily anything for you to learn from the comment. A comment like this says much more about the person who made it than it does about you.

Sometimes, a person might be making hurtful comments because they are feeling jealous of you.[2] Perhaps a classmate is saying unkind things to you about your outfit, but it's not really because they don't like your clothes – **quite the opposite**! They might just be saying those mean things to cover up the fact that they wish they had an outfit as cool as yours. If you find yourself in this sort of situation, keeping this in mind can help you to move on from any sad feelings you're experiencing. After all,

---

[2] My brother once made fun of me by being mean about my failed attempts at teleporting. Years later, I realized that he couldn't teleport at all, and he'd just been jealous that I could even half do it (even if I didn't always end up where I was aiming to go!).

what's the point in being sad about someone being mean because they really want to be like you?

Unfortunately, sometimes it's people who we thought were our friends who make these sorts of mean comments because they are jealous. If you have a friend who is saying these sorts of things to you, it might be time to consider whether that friend is a good person to have in your life. There might be other things going on that could help explain why they are acting this way, such as difficulties at home. Deciding to end a friendship can be a big decision, so it's a good idea to **talk to somebody you trust about what is happening first**.

NOT YOUR FIGHT

Sometimes you might find yourself facing negative comments or emotions that aren't directly aimed at you, but that you still feel confused, angry, sad or scared about. Perhaps your parents have separated and argue in front of you a lot, or maybe some of your best friends are in a fight and you're stuck in the middle. If people you love aren't getting along with one another, you shouldn't feel as though you have to choose sides. This is especially true if it's your parents – you should never be involved in their arguments. It's their fight, not yours, so you don't need to say or do anything.

You do, however, have the right to voice your feelings, and it's important to have someone you can talk to honestly about how you feel, whether that's a friend, family member, teacher or a counsellor. You might worry that you will upset someone if you say what you really think – for example, that you wish your parents would just stop fighting – but your feelings matter too. When someone else listens to you, they are acknowledging that your feelings are real and important. Just knowing that you have been heard can help you to feel stronger and less like you have no say in the situation.

Also, if your parents are fighting, know that this doesn't change their feelings for you. They love you and care for you as much as ever. Even though some things in your life might change, your parents' love for you is one thing that won't.

If it's your friends who are fighting, then you have a choice about how you handle it. One thing you might do is try to help your friends remember why they were friends in the first place. You could also simply stay out of it – you don't need to feel like it's your job to fix their friendship.

When negative things happen that bring big changes to your life, it can be helpful to keep some of your routines the same, if you can. This includes continuing to do some of the things that you and just one of your parents or friends enjoy doing together. For example, you and your mum might like going to sports games together, so just the two of you can keep doing that. It's OK to enjoy yourself with just one person at a time. You don't always have to do everything together.

Keeping some familiar routines and activities going can help things to feel a little more stable, and will remind you that life can and will carry on. In this way, a familiar routine can be reassuring and help you to engage your regeneration superpower to begin to heal!

HEALING

Sometimes, people or pets who we care about very much pass away. This can be an extremely difficult thing to experience, and you might feel very sad because the person or pet is no longer physically around. Often, how close you were to this person or pet will have an impact on how much you are affected by not having them around any more. You may have known that you were going to have to say goodbye to them, or perhaps no one expected it and it came as a shock. Experiencing a period of shock is normal if it was sudden, because your brain is busy trying to process everything.

It is perfectly normal to feel sad and angry in this sort of situation. The emotions that you feel show that you cared very much for the person or pet you have lost. It will be a difficult time, but doing

INNER HERO

Look at photos from a time with happy memories.

things like making sure you eat regularly, go to bed at a normal time and spend time with other people you love can help.

If you do lose someone you love, you may have lots of worries and questions in your head. You might wonder if it was your fault, or whether you could have done things differently. You might even try to work out why this happened to you. Although these thoughts are very common, please remember that it is not your fault. Having someone to talk to about your loss can help you to deal with these feelings. Perhaps you can talk to someone at home, or even a teacher or a counsellor at school.

Every culture and religion deals with loss in its own way. When someone dies, it is common to hold a ceremony to celebrate that person's life and the impact that they had on the world. This ceremony gives people a chance to begin working through their own loss and sadness, and it also brings everyone together to support each other. People around you may want to talk about their memories of the person who has died. You might find it difficult to talk about them at first, especially if everyone around you is sad – but remembering good times by sharing stories and looking at photos can be a way to activate your regeneration superpower! It can help you to feel connected to those around you, and less alone. Sharing stories can be a source of support for everyone.

To begin with, it is normal to think about the person or pet you have lost a lot. You may feel very sad because you miss them. And, as time goes on, it's also OK when you start to think about them a bit less. Eventually, you may reach the point where you can go for a while without thinking about them – then suddenly something happens that reminds you of them. This can be tough and take you by surprise, but it's important to remember that no reaction is a bad one. Everybody handles loss in different ways, and there is no right way to do it. Once again, just try to make sure that you are taking care of yourself and not spending too much time alone.

Immediately after you lose your loved one, you might feel as though your life will never be the same again. While it may not be exactly the same, with time you will start to heal and to enjoy life again. At times of loss, which result in massive changes, it can be helpful if some things in your life stay unchanged. For example, you might find it helps to continue going to school and seeing your friends. Carrying on doing these things can be a powerful tool for engaging your regeneration superpower, because it reminds you that some things haven't changed. This can help you to feel safe, and reassure you that life will carry on in some way, even if you don't quite feel ready for it to.

HEALTHY HEALING

At any time of pain, some of us may stop looking after ourselves properly. We might not get enough sleep, not go out for fresh air or not eat the right foods. In order to heal from any sort of pain, it is important to take care of yourself and your body, even if you don't really feel like it.

Making an effort to do things you used to enjoy can help you to feel happy and give you a chance to start healing. Sometimes, your brain might process feelings of pain and sadness as anger. If you do feel angry, that's perfectly normal. One way to work through the anger is by exercising, because it can give your body a way to release your feelings.

If you are struggling to sleep, it can help to spend some time focusing on your body when you are lying in bed at night. Start by focusing on your toes for about ten seconds – really concentrate on relaxing each one of them. Then, relax your feet, then your ankles, and slowly move upwards through each part of your body. Pay attention to how each part feels – for instance, is it hot or cold?

Another way that some people find helps them to wind down at the end of the day is listening to relaxing music or audiobooks. One thing you want to avoid is spending time looking at your phone or computer screen right before bed – the light that screens give off wakes your brain up, and will make it difficult for you to get a good night's sleep.

Since you can't necessarily control your regeneration, it can be a difficult superpower to engage, especially because it's one you use during tough times. Regardless of the situation, just remember that there is no right or wrong way to process any form of sadness or pain. You can cry or smile. Just cut yourself some slack, and take one day at a time. At the same time, make sure that you take care of yourself and that you talk to others about what you're going through. Your friends and loved ones still care about you, so don't feel as though you have to handle anything on your own.

OUTER HERO

Think of a big event that has made someone's life harder.
Could you do anything to help them?

Invincibility is one of the coolest powers a superhero can have! It basically means you can't be harmed. Now, tell me one person who wouldn't want that ability!

You may believe that this is the sort of power that you're just born with or get,[1] but it's actually something you have to work towards. People often confuse strength and invincibility, but they're not quite the same thing. Yes, super strength is important (in fact, I've written a whole other chapter on it!), but invincibility is something else.

Invincibility isn't about being invulnerable to bullets. What it's really about is resisting feelings of self-doubt and learning not to pay attention to unhelpful comments and judgement. Essentially, invincibility can be broken down into two categories: handling negativity, and growing your confidence. You'll become more powerful by being able to handle negative things, and when your confidence grows you'll tip right over the edge into total invincibility!

In this chapter, you're going to learn how to become invincible to negativity and judgement. The truth is that this superpower comes from within – you already have it all inside you. Now, let's bring it out!

---

[1] I'm thinking a Spider-Man radioactive-spider type situation here.

THE POWER OF POSITIVITY

Self-doubt is an example of negativity, and it can show itself in many ways. One of the most common, of course, is when you doubt your own abilities, especially when trying new things. You might be a bit of a cautious person to begin with, so trying anything different from what you are used to feels a bit unnatural and difficult.

Self-doubt can sometimes sound a bit like these thoughts.

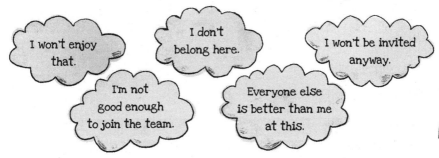

I won't enjoy that.

I don't belong here.

I won't be invited anyway.

I'm not good enough to join the team.

Everyone else is better than me at this.

Sound familiar? If so, you're not the only one who has these sorts of doubts. Everyone has them! I know it might sound ridiculous, but even the most confident people sometimes think they aren't good enough.[2] Your personality and your

INNER HERO

For every negative thought you have, try to counteract it with two positive thoughts.

---

[2] Even Captain Marvel doubts herself every once in a while, and she's one of the most powerful superheroes of them all!

previous experiences can also have an effect on whether or not you have negative thoughts, so if you do feel down sometimes don't beat yourself up.

Negative thoughts can be really pushy! They can become so loud in your head that they feel overwhelming. They might sometimes be so noisy that you feel as though you can't concentrate at school, or you don't feel hungry, or you don't want to see your friends. These are all signs that you need to ask for some extra help. Did you know that part of being invincible is knowing when to ask for help? When you notice that you are feeling overwhelmed and then get the support to fight back,

INNER HERO

List three things you like about yourself and say them out loud every morning.

you're really putting your invincibility superpower to use! Think about it: both the Avengers and Justice League work together as a team, right? Exactly.

In fact, learning how to notice when negative thoughts are popping into your head is the first step towards becoming invincible. There are loads of ways to do this, but one of the easiest is to wear something on your wrist that you move to the opposite wrist every time you notice a negative thought.[3] Try this for a few days, and see if it gets easier to notice the negative thoughts. Don't worry, though – knowing that the thoughts are there and what they are is not the same as listening to or believing in them. You just need to know when they are happening to be able to move on to the second step in developing your superpower!

The second step towards becoming invincible is learning how to challenge these thoughts. When you notice yourself experiencing a negative thought, stop and ask yourself the following questions.

- **Is there any evidence that the thought is true?**
- **Is this thought fact or is it my opinion?**
- **What are the facts?**
- **What would I say to a friend who was in the same situation?**

Most likely, once you've answered these questions, you'll be able to see a way to fight the self-doubt. For example, you might notice that you've been thinking that you're bad at football.

---

[3] My brother and I did this with elastic bands. We may or may not have pinged each other's wrists . . . a lot. We also may or may not have got grounded for it.

However, when you stop and consider the questions above, you might remind yourself that you score the second-highest number of goals each week in PE class – so it's fair to say there isn't any evidence that you're bad at football! On the other hand, if you score the second-lowest number of goals, then instead of thinking 'I'm not good enough', you could argue back, 'I will get better with practice.'[4]

---

[4] I tried thinking this without actually practising, and just ended up having to quit the League of Gymnastic Superheroes because I didn't get any better. Now they are the galaxy champions and I just watch them on TV.

Here's a story about Taylor. She had just started a new school and the cricket try-outs were being held in four weeks. Taylor had been on the cricket team at her previous school, but here there was much more competition. She was good at cricket and loved to play on a team, but what if the other students were better than her?

She had even heard a rumour that one student played for the county! Taylor started wondering whether she should even try out at all. What was the point if she already knew the other students were better than her?

Fortunately, Taylor was learning how to be a superhero, just like you. She was full of self-doubt, but she knew she needed to stop and think before she made any decisions. She put her invincibility into action. First, she made a list of the facts. She asked herself, 'What do I actually know about the situation?' Here's what she worked out.

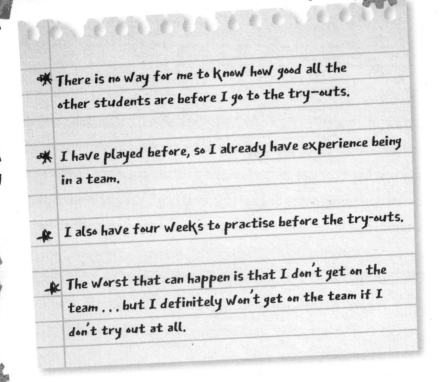

* There is no way for me to know how good all the other students are before I go to the try-outs.

* I have played before, so I already have experience being in a team.

* I also have four weeks to practise before the try-outs.

* The worst that can happen is that I don't get on the team . . . but I definitely won't get on the team if I don't try out at all.

Taylor realized she had a choice. She could either let the negative thoughts stop her from trying out for the team, or she could use her invincibility to push past them. She reminded herself that the only way to know whether she was good enough to make the team was to try out, plus she had four whole weeks to practise!

INNER HERO

Practise a confident pose in the mirror. Stand up straight, shoulders back and make good eye contact.

NO NEED FOR NEGATIVITY

Sometimes, the negative thoughts might not come from inside your own head. Sometimes, they can come from other people. If someone in your life is doing or saying negative things, you can use your invincibility superpower to ignore them – or even to help them!

Occasionally, other people will say or do things that aren't very nice, and as a result you might start to doubt yourself. Some examples of this sort of thing are when someone:

- **talks down to you, or thinks you don't understand things**
- **makes you feel bad and criticizes you**
- **says negative things about other people you know**
- **tries to control who you hang out with.**

If you have someone in your life who is doing any of these things, it's important to surround yourself instead with other people who will boost your confidence and make you feel more positive. You might need to consider whether that person is the right person for you to be spending lots of time around.

Also, although you can't control how others behave, you do have a right to expect certain things, such as being listened to and respected. You also have the right to say no to things you don't want to do or don't agree with – and so do others! This can make things a bit confusing if you don't agree with someone else on something, but it's important to remember that it's OK to disagree. Listening to another person's opinion isn't the same as agreeing with it – but you do need to listen. After all, your thoughts and needs deserve to be heard, and so do the thoughts of others. The trick is to find the balance between listening to another person's opinion and weighing up whether or not you have to act on it.

If you do disagree with someone, a good way to think of things is to imagine how you would like to be treated if the situation was the other way round, and they were disagreeing with you. Do you like it when others try to force their views on to you? Or do you prefer it when they make an effort to calmly explain their thoughts? It's rarely helpful to try to push your opinion on to someone else. Instead of trying to convince them to think the same thing as you, focus on helping them to understand what you're saying. Staying calm, avoiding raising your voice, taking turns to speak and listening to others can help in achieving this.

It's also possible that the person being negative might not be doing it intentionally to upset you, but actually needs your help. Many people don't realize that they are being negative – you might even have done this to someone else at some point (lots of us have). Sometimes, people say or do negative things to others because they are experiencing their own self-doubt. They just say the things they think about themselves to other people. If this is what is happening, maybe you could teach this person how to engage their own invincibility? Once you've mastered your own superpower, you could show them how to fight back against their bad thoughts! As always, true superheroes use their powers for good.

BE UNBREAKABLE

So, we've covered the first part of invincibility, which is fighting negativity. Now it's time for the rest: being confident! When you believe in yourself, you're at your strongest. So, let's turn our attention to believing in ourselves, to acknowledging our uniqueness and realizing what we can achieve when we embrace our differences.

INNER HERO

Learn about a new faith, religion or culture by talking to friends, asking an adult to help you look on the internet or get some books from your local library.

There are over seven billion people on this planet and every single one of us is unique. Even identical twins don't have identical fingerprints. How cool is that? We live in a world full of difference, and each and every difference is like its own mini superpower. It's the things that are unique about each of us that make us strong and special! What's more, differences aren't just things like your hairstyle, hobbies or the clothes you wear. The world is full of different languages, religions, traditions, genders, lifestyles . . . The list goes on!

Differences are cool. They're what make our world the wonderful, interesting, inspiring place it is. When you understand this, you can embrace your own uniqueness for the special and powerful thing it is. At the same time, you can do the same for other people. You can make an effort to learn about other people's experiences – and, especially, how those experiences differ from your own. When you accept and embrace your own differences, it naturally follows that you'll accept others' differences, and it's by doing this that you'll start to understand more about yourself and about the world you live in. Pretty neat, huh?

Now, I want you to think of something about you that makes you stand out. Is there something about you that no one else has? Something that makes you special? I'm sure you can think of plenty of things![5] Make a list of all these things that make you different, then alongside each thing note something positive about that thing. For instance, perhaps you're the tallest kid in your class? Well, that's pretty cool – it might mean that you can see further than anyone else or reach things that others can't! Or maybe you have a name that no one else in your class has?

---

[5] Sometimes, I think I'm pretty boring, then I remember all the ways I'm different from people I know – including my family! Like how I can sort of sometimes teleport, but my brother can't . . . Oh, did I already mention that?

I know that it can sometimes be hard to see your differences as a good thing, but it's important to make an effort to see the positives. When you do, you'll start appreciating your uniqueness. This is a huge part of becoming more confident. Plus, how boring would the world be if we were all the same?

When you list all of your differences and their positives like this, you'll see that they come together to give you the building blocks of being unbreakable. They'll act as a barrier against anyone who might be negative towards you. It doesn't matter what anyone else thinks of your differences. All that matters is that you know they're a positive and important part of who you are!

As you learn to pay less attention to the negative opinions of others, you'll also start to show the real you. You'll become more confident about sharing who you are and what you think – although this is one of those things that can take a bit of practice and time to get the hang of. Being assertive and voicing your opinions can be especially tricky if your personality means you naturally try to avoid upsetting or angering others. But, even if this is you, it's no good keeping your feelings to yourself simply to save the feelings of others, because you'll possibly just end up feeling annoyed and unheard. This is why it's important to learn how to confidently – and calmly – communicate your opinions and feelings.

Of course, it's usually a bit easier to share your opinions when you're around people you know and feel comfortable with. Friends and family who love and support you can help you to develop the confidence to speak up. One way to become more confident in your opinions is to try using 'I' statements when you're with others. What I mean by this is to avoid saying, 'Maybe we could go to the park . . .' Instead, try saying, 'I think we should go to the park.' See how the people you are with react. Do they listen to you more? When you're doing this, remember that politeness is still important! Make sure you say things in a way that you'd like someone else to say them to you.

One of the really great things about feeling positive and confident is that it helps to release loads of happy chemicals called endorphins into your body. These chemicals can help new things seem less scary and also make you feel amazing![6] One of the ways to really boost these chemicals is to make sure you take time out of your day to show yourself some kindness. Here are a few ideas.

SET YOURSELF A SMALL DAILY GOAL.

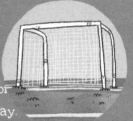

This will help you learn what you're really capable of! For example, you could make your bed every morning or aim to finish your homework by a certain time every day.

BE NICE TO YOURSELF.

Learn to accept compliments from others by kindly saying 'thank you', rather than disagreeing.[7]

---

[6] You just know that Kamala Khan has endless endorphins!

[7] I once saved Earth from being hit by an asteroid by punching the asteroid into pieces. It was pretty cool. When people complimented me for it, I could hardly argue, could I? It would have been rude!

LOOK CONFIDENT.

Pay attention to how you stand and what you wear. Imagining yourself being confident is actually a big step towards making it happen. Even if you don't feel confident inside, you can pretend that you do, and nobody else will know the difference from the outside. Fake it till you make it!

When you truly start to feel confident, that's when you become unbreakable! The goal isn't so much to get what you want as it is to simply say what you want and why.

OUTER HERO

Join a debating team or set one up at your school.

Invincibility can seem like it's a solo game, but actually it's a team effort – everyone is stronger when they work together to build each other up! Being part of a team can really help you to develop confidence. Can you think of a time when you were part of a team that worked well together?

Was there something about the team that made it easy for you all to communicate with one another? When we're part of a team that works well together, we can take the things we learn from the team and apply it to ourselves. It teaches us so much about confidence: we learn to share ideas and listen to others, and how to communicate our feelings and opinions. It even teaches us how to make compromises when we need to, so that we can make sure there are benefits for everyone involved and not just ourselves.

GOALS ARE THE GOAT!

As your invincibility superpower grows, you'll find yourself feeling more confident and you might want to try new things and set goals to become the best version of yourself. You'll want to be the GOAT![8]

But it's often hard to know where to start. Luckily, it's not hard to find out! First, think about your hobbies and interests, then ask yourself the following questions.

- **Does one hobby or interest in particular stand out? Maybe playing the piano or being in the netball team?**
- **Is there something I would like to achieve that relates to that hobby or interest? Passing grade 4 piano perhaps? Or scoring more goals?**
- **Can I make a plan to achieve it?**

---

[8] Who doesn't want to be the GOAT? Aiming to be the Greatest Of All Time is what I'm trying to do, but we're all friends here, so let's share the title!

The answer to that last one is yes! You can create a plan to achieve your goals! I'm here to show you exactly how to do that. Coming up with a plan can help to make your goal feel more achievable, and you can create a plan by breaking things down into the following four steps – which actually spell the word 'goal' (convenient, huh?).

1. GOALS:

What would you like to achieve? Is there a way to measure if you've achieved it?

2. OBSTACLES:

Is there anything that could stop you from achieving your goal? Do you need something in order to reach your goal? Is there anyone who can help you to get it?

3. ATTITUDE:

Nothing worth doing is easy! You will need to stay positive and focused to achieve your goal.

4. LEARNING:

It's OK to make mistakes. In fact, it's a good thing, so long as you use the mistake to learn what to do differently next time.

Of course, the first step is setting your goal. Do you remember the story about Taylor's cricket try-outs? Her goal was to feel confident enough to try out for the team. It wasn't necessarily to get on to the team – that was something that may or may not happen, outside of Taylor's control. However, so long as Taylor practised hard and followed her plan, she would go to the try-outs knowing she'd done her very best. And that's worth celebrating as an achievement!

INNER HERO

Think of three things you've done this week that you are proud of.

Can you think of a time when you felt particularly confident? Maybe you stood up in class and answered a question, or perhaps you scored a goal in a hockey game. Was there anything you'd done that helped you to feel confident? Maybe you had already read about the topic, or had practised scoring goals in your lunch break. Identifying the things that can help you to feel good about yourself will give you some tools for overcoming any obstacles in your way. This is an important part of learning to use your invincibility.

There's one thing that every superhero who knows how to use their invincibility superpower has in common. It's something they do regularly, and it helps them to feel more prepared and confident. Do you know what it is? Yep, you got it! Practice. A powerful way to adjust your attitude towards failure is to see every mistake as an opportunity to practise. When you look at things like this, you'll see that making a mistake is actually taking another step towards success. In fact, mistakes teach us two very important things: each mistake helps you to work out what things you find difficult and need to focus on, and every mistake helps you to understand that you can get better.

The more you practise something, the more your brain learns to do that thing automatically. Positive thinking is great and can give us the confidence we need to try in the first place, but it's no replacement for practice, practice, practice!

Take a look at the following picture. Now, tell me: who is the more likely to achieve their dream?

INVINCIBLE ISN'T UNBEATABLE

As you will have realized by now, becoming invincible takes some effort and persistence. You have to really want it. This means carrying on even when you don't succeed at something the first time round.

When you see a successful person looking like they do everything easily, it's important to remember that what you're not seeing is all the mistakes they made in order to get to where they are. They got good at what they do because they kept trying . . . and tried again and again and again! So, next time you see someone doing really well – be it a pop star performing their latest hit or

Darren from Class C3 winning every competition on sports day –
think of how hard they must have practised to get there. If you do
this, something magical might just happen: you may feel happy
for them, rather than sad or envious. You could also talk to them
about how they achieved their goals. As you know by now, working
together is always better for everyone. It's certainly better than
being jealous!

There are so many parts to becoming invincible that it might
sometimes feel like an impossible goal, but it's all about trying,
failing and trying again. Go out there, be confident and set yourself
some goals to work towards. You're only as invincible as your
mistakes make you!

CONTROL THE ELEMENTS: EARTH AND AIR

Earth and air come as a package. They are two things that surround us every single day, but we pay almost no attention to them. Do you spend much time thinking about the air you're breathing in? What about the ground beneath you? I bet you are now that I've mentioned them, but if you don't usually pay any attention that's OK. It's not your fault. There's so much to take in all around us that it's impossible to take it all in all the time!

Your air power and earth power are linked, just like the elements themselves. Your earth power will help you to grow your kindness by feeding and nurturing it until it blossoms into something sustainable – and healthy! – for the world around it. You'll then use your air power to apply this kindness to the things around you that you can't see or touch – things like the environment and people on the other side of the world who you've never met!

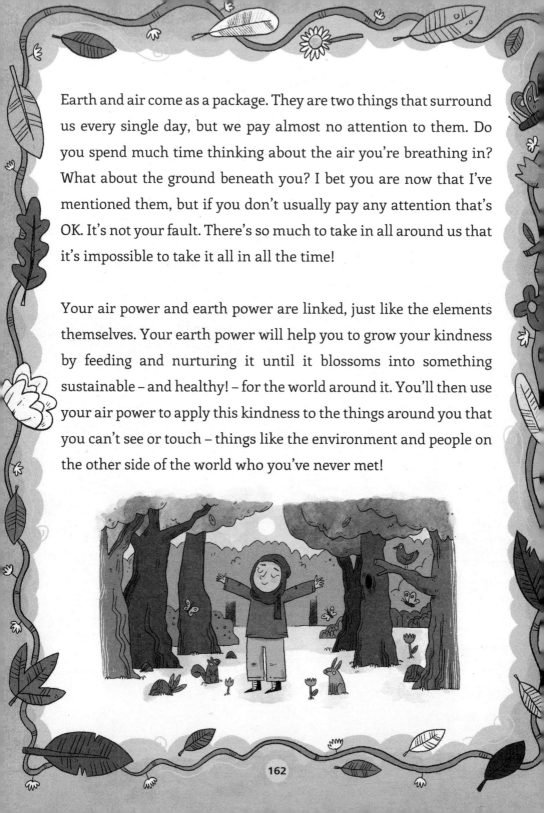

SOW THE SEEDS OF KINDNESS

Caring for others is something you might already do every day without realizing it. Perhaps you helped a friend tidy up at school, or you made a cake for someone's birthday? Enhancing your earth power is all about taking this kindness to the next level by spreading it far and wide.

We can begin to develop our earth power by showing kindness through the way we act. Think of all the different people you cross paths with every day – for example, the person who scans the food at the supermarket check-out, the person who empties your rubbish bins, or the person who helps you cross the road outside school.[1] You may already feel grateful to these people, but a simple and small act of kindness like saying 'thank you' lets them know you value their work. After all, wouldn't you want

INNER HERO

Think of something positive about each person you interact with today.

---

[1] I did this the other day. Did you see me? I waved at you!

someone to say thank you if you did something nice for them? This is one of the easiest ways to be kind, but it's something you might need to remind yourself to do. Why not try doing it every day for a week? Do people smile at you more? (I bet they do!) Every time you perform a small act of kindness like this, you make someone else's day that little bit better.

Once you feel like you're nailing the kindness game, it's time to start growing your new power even more! The next step is to understand when others are being unkind, and learn how to react in those situations. It's important to flex your empathy muscles when detecting if something isn't fair or nice.[2]

Here's a story about Bruno. One day, Bruno walked over to a group of his friends at lunchtime and heard them talking about a classmate, Rose. They were saying that they didn't like Rose's new haircut, and were making jokes about how she looked. It would have been easy for Bruno to join in, especially if he hadn't liked

---

[2] If you've read the chapter on your telepathy superpower, you'll already know all about empathy! If not, or if you need a reminder, empathy is when you make an effort to understand and imagine how another person is feeling.

her haircut either.[3] But Bruno thought about how he would feel if he heard people talking about him in the same way, and he knew it would hurt his feelings. He looked over and saw Rose sitting a few seats away. She looked upset, and he realized she might have been able to overhear everything that her classmates were saying!

So, instead of joining in, Bruno did the following things.

- **He asked his friends how they would feel if they heard people saying unkind things about them.**
- **He suggested they change the conversation to a new topic.**
- **Then he went over to sit with Rose and ate his lunch with her.**

---

[3] The number of times I've thought my sidekick's costume looks a bit silly . . . but then I remember that other people think the same about my underpants-on-the-outside situation. So who am I to judge?

It's never OK to do or say things that are hurtful to others, whether through unkind words, physically hurting someone or by purposely ignoring them and leaving them out. You might not be able to control other people's behaviour, but you can always choose not to join in with hurtful actions. Sometimes, people don't act in the best way. If you see someone being cruel towards or bullying someone else, or if you're being bullied yourself, tell someone you trust and who can help stop it, such as a teacher or parent.

OUTER HERO

Pay someone a compliment that will give them a confidence boost!

Don't participate in unkind behaviour. Instead, use your earth power to sow the seeds of kindness. You can do this by setting a positive example through your own words and actions. Likewise, if you notice someone else doing something nice, that's their earth power showing itself! Just like a plant, that seed of kindness needs water to grow. You can feed it with encouragement and reassurance to help it blossom.

WAVE YOUR KINDNESS IN THE AIR LIKE YOU JUST DON'T CARE!

Just like your earth power, you use your air power to show kindness – but the main difference is that you use your air power to show kindness to the world that you can't necessarily see.

I know that sounds a bit weird, but what I mean is that there is actually an entire world outside of the one that you know and see every day. Although there's lots that's beautiful about this world, there are also things that aren't always so great about it – that's why we need superheroes like you! For starters, not everyone in the world has the same things that everyone else has – things like enough food and clothing, a warm house, or a loving family. (And then there's the actual physical world that we live in – you know, that little thing called the Earth – which is full of amazing things, but which humans aren't always very respectful of or careful with. We're going to talk about that shortly!)

INNER HERO

Volunteer with your friends or family to clean up or look after a local park.

Here's something I know you'll be happy to hear: your air power is actually one of the easiest superpowers to master.

When it comes to using it to show kindness by helping others who you don't know or who don't even live in the same country, there are loads of different things, big and small, that you can do. It could be something as simple as donating your old clothes to charity or giving food to a local homeless shelter or food bank.

What's more, your air power doesn't always have be about giving away physical items or things that cost money, either. Giving some of your time to support a good cause is another brilliant way to help others. If you love animals, maybe you could volunteer at a local animal shelter? Or, if you're wild about nature, why not try helping out at a local park event to clear up the green spaces around you?

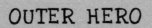

Help others in need by donating cans of food to your local food bank.

You can also hold or participate in events to raise donations to support an important cause. For instance, you could organize a collection or charity drive among your friends or classmates.[4]

If you feel strongly about a particular issue, and you want to raise awareness about it, you could ask an adult or teacher to help you find out about local youth forums, or even national and international ones. These are groups that encourage young people to voice their opinions, for example by writing to their local MPs or councillors.

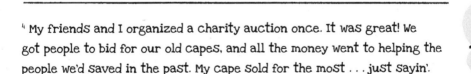

[4] My friends and I organized a charity auction once. It was great! We got people to bid for our old capes, and all the money went to helping the people we'd saved in the past. My cape sold for the most . . . just sayin'.

Be creative! There are so many ways that you can help others. If you need more ideas, try talking to your family or a teacher about how you can help others. Most adults will love what you're trying to do and will be super happy to help.

Just like smiling, kindness is contagious. The more kindness you give out, the more you will receive in return. Taking small steps to do things for others every day doesn't just help other people to feel good, either – you'll soon notice how good it makes you feel, too. We all deserve to live in a fair and equal world. When you notice unfairness and take a stand to help others, you're helping to make the world a better place for everyone. And if that's not what a superhero does, then I don't know what is!

PROTECTING THE WORLD

The superhero code says that we need to protect the world, right? Well, you've learned how to do that for the people who live in the world, but that's only part of the job. Being a superhero means protecting the actual planet too – sometimes from ourselves.

You probably already know a little bit about climate change, or global warming as it's also called. It's a bit scary actually, as it basically means that the Earth's atmosphere is gradually getting warmer. This is a problem because the rising temperature is causing ice to melt in some places and sea levels to rise in others, which has been extremely harmful to both people and animals living in certain parts of the world. The change in temperature also means that some places now get less rain than they once did, which can be bad for growing food. Meanwhile, it also means that other places now get more rain, which can cause floods and other types of extreme weather.

According to scientists, climate change is caused by things that humans do every day to pollute the world around us – things like using electricity, driving cars and even eating meat. We all need somewhere to live, and at the moment the Earth is the only place we've got, so we need to clean up our act and start taking better care of it. If we want to reduce the negative impact that humans are having on the planet, we all need to make an effort to change our habits.

This is an important global challenge. Are you up to it? I think you are!

This world we live in provides us with everything we need to stay alive, so it's only fair that we should pay it back, right?

Let's look at a few ways that you can look after the planet and show it some love.

REUSE OR RECYCLE

Make an effort to reuse things as much as you can. For example, take reusable bags with you if you do the supermarket shopping with your family, try to make your clothes last until you grow out of them instead of buying new ones, and if you take your lunch to school with you pack it in reusable lunch boxes and wrappers.

If you can't reuse something, try to recycle it.

When you recycle materials, it means they can be used more than once, so fewer new materials are needed to make new products. Usually, you can find a separate type of bin outside your house for rubbish that can be recycled. Loads of stuff can go in there, including glass, certain plastics and cardboard. These days, it's becoming really cool to reuse things. Lots of fashionable people buy their clothes from charity shops, which is awesome because it reuses something but also because it means no one else will ever have the same clothes as you! It's win–win!

As a general rule, it's best to try to use as little plastic as you can. Not all plastics can be recycled, and a large amount of plastic ends up in the sea, which is really harmful to wildlife. You can make small steps towards using less plastic by putting leftover food in reusable containers instead of using cling film, and by taking your reusable bags when you go shopping instead of using single-use plastic ones.

REPURPOSE

Many things we use every day can also be used for other things. The internet is full of repurposing ideas! There are videos online that'll tell you how to do everything from make a cat bed out of an old T-shirt to turning an old peanut-butter jar into a pencil holder. You can find a new purpose for almost everything, and that means you won't need to throw it away. Instead, you might just find a new hobby and craft something cool!

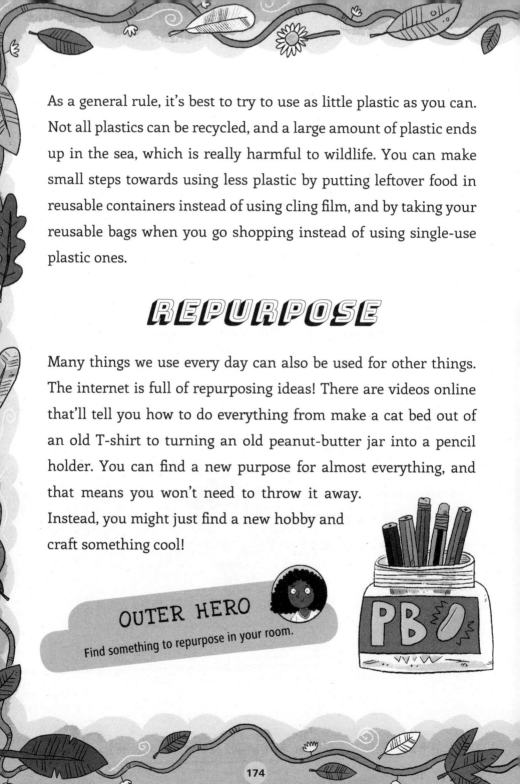

OUTER HERO

Find something to repurpose in your room.

SAVE ELECTRICITY

We use energy in the form of electricity every day to do things like power our lights, watch television, use our computers and to heat our water. It's easy to forget that these things have an impact on the world around us, but they do. Many of the energy sources we depend on, such as gas and coal, are in limited supply. It took the Earth millions of years to make the amount we have now. Energy sources like this are pretty bad for the environment. Better sources of energy are solar power (from the sun) or wind power. You might not personally be able to find good sources of energy for your home, but you can reduce how much energy you use simply by turning off the lights when you leave a room, flicking off power switches and by having shorter showers.

TRAVEL SMART

Reducing how much you use a car to get around the place isn't just great for the planet – it's also an easy way to get in some exercise! Cars burn fuel, which is a bad energy source, and put a lot of pollution into the air. This is why it's good to cycle or walk, if you can, instead of driving. If you take longer journeys with your family, why not suggest taking public transport instead of the car? It could be a fun adventure, and you might even discover that it's better than taking the car.

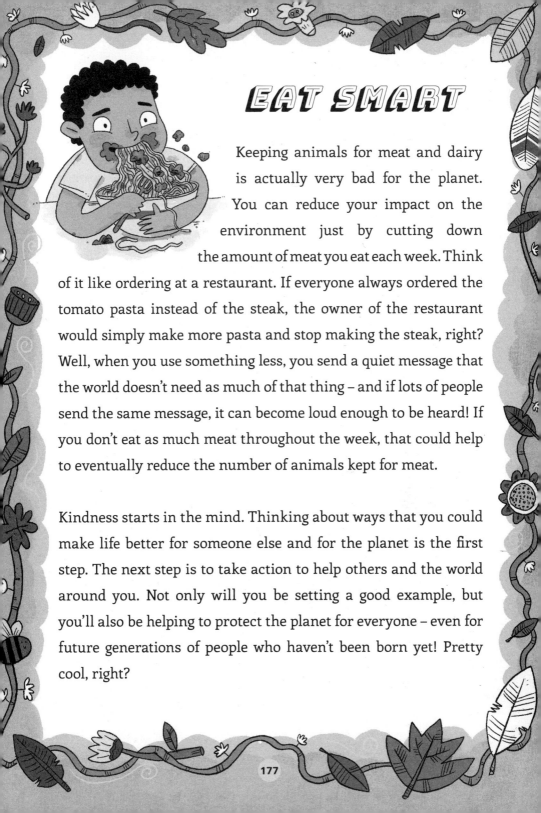

EAT SMART

Keeping animals for meat and dairy is actually very bad for the planet. You can reduce your impact on the environment just by cutting down the amount of meat you eat each week. Think of it like ordering at a restaurant. If everyone always ordered the tomato pasta instead of the steak, the owner of the restaurant would simply make more pasta and stop making the steak, right? Well, when you use something less, you send a quiet message that the world doesn't need as much of that thing – and if lots of people send the same message, it can become loud enough to be heard! If you don't eat as much meat throughout the week, that could help to eventually reduce the number of animals kept for meat.

Kindness starts in the mind. Thinking about ways that you could make life better for someone else and for the planet is the first step. The next step is to take action to help others and the world around you. Not only will you be setting a good example, but you'll also be helping to protect the planet for everyone – even for future generations of people who haven't been born yet! Pretty cool, right?

You've worked hard to train your powers and now it's time to become everything you were meant to be! Remember this is just the beginning because your powers can always grow, and the best way to learn is by doing . . . so it's time to go out there and . . .

BE YOUR OWN SUPERHERO!

A NOTE FROM THE AUTHOR

I hope that many of the ideas and actions in this book will help you feel stronger and more confident in your daily life. But part of being a true superhero is also knowing when you need support from others.

If you think you could have a problem with your mental health, talk to your parent, teacher or another adult you trust. You might be able to find more support if you need it through your GP, a school counsellor or a mental health service. I'm also including a list of helpful resources which might help you to understand and manage what you are experiencing.

CHILDLINE

www.childline.org.uk

A free, private and confidential service for young people under the age of 19, where you can talk about anything, whatever your worry, whenever you need help.

Call: 0800 1111

KOOTH

www.kooth.com

An online counselling and emotional well-being platform for children and young people. The site includes on online chat feature, staffed by trained counsellors, and you can also read articles written by other young people who have experienced their own difficulties.

CALM HARM

www.calmharm.co.uk

Calm Harm is an award-winning app which is based on the principles of Dialectical Behaviour Therapy (DBT). It provides tasks to help young people cope with urges to self-harm and has been recommended by the NHS.

NSPCC

www.nspcc.org.uk

The leading children's charity in the UK, specializing in child protection and dedicated to the fight for every childhood. Their specialists are available 24/7, 365 days a year.

Adults helpline: 0808 800 5000
Children and young people helpline, Childline: 0800 1111

YOUNG MINDS

www.youngminds.org.uk

A leading charity that fights for children and young people's mental health. Their website offers advice on coping with mental health issues. They also offer a 24/7 text service to help young people experiencing a mental health crisis.

YoungMinds Crisis Messenger: text 'YM' to 85258

FAMILY LIVES

www.familylives.org.uk

A national charity that specializes in professional, non-judgemental support and advice for families. Nearly all their services are free and they can be contacted 365 days a year.

Call: 0808 800 2222

SAMARITANS

www.samaritans.org

The organization that offers a totally anonymous, nonreligious and confidential crisis line to provide non-judgemental, emotional support to anyone feeling down or desperate. Available for free 24/7, 365 days a year.

Call: 116 123
Email: jo@samaritans.org

FRANK

www.talktofrank.com

The national drugs charity that provides comprehensive information about drugs and offers free confidential support and advice 24/7, 365 days a year.

Call: 0300 123 6600
Text: 82111

MIND

www.mind.org.uk

A mental health charity that aims to empower anyone experiencing a mental health problem by providing advice and support, to make sure that no one has to face these problems alone.

Mind Infoline (weekdays 9 a.m.–6 p.m.): 0300 123 3393
Text: 86463

PAPYRUS

www.papyrus-uk.org

The national charity working to give hope to young people under the age of 35 and to prevent young suicide. They provide confidential support and advice to vulnerable young people or those concerned about their loved ones.

HopelineUK: 0800 068 41 41
(weekdays 10 a.m.–10 p.m.; weekends 2 p.m.–10 p.m.)

MINDMATE

www.mindmate.org.uk

MindMate is a website created in Leeds, England but is freely accessible to anyone and offers advice on difficulties such as coping with stress, worry, self-image and anger.

Shout crisis text line: 85258